Jungian Archetypal Psychology
Made Easy

(We Promise)

By Theresa Bauer, LPC, CAC III
and Elizabeth Cox M. A.
with Charles Bebeau
Illustrated by Sarah Trumpp

First published by AuthorHouse 06/30/04

ISBN: 1-4184-6522-4 (e-book)
ISBN: 1-4184-3009-9 (Paperback)

Printed in the United States of America
Bloomington, IN

This book is printed on acid free paper.

Table of Contents

Introduction

This book is divided into four sections. The first section describes Jungian Archetypal Psychology as developed by Charles Bebeau, Ph.D. The second section is a description of the 12 archetypes, with 12 illustrations by Sarah Trumpp. There is also a little play/scenario to further illustrate and bring to life these archetypes that live in all of us. The third section by Elizabeth Cox describes how Jungian Archetypal Psychology can be used in a therapeutic setting with the Archetype of the Mystic.

The fourth section describes how to use an astrological chart to determine one's ruling archetypes (we all have 4,5, or 6 ruling archetypes). I find that some people really enjoy working with a symbol system such as astrology, where other people find it too complex or uninteresting. You can understand the archetypes without reading the fourth section or understanding astrology at all. But for those readers who have some understanding of astrology or who would like to learn, we offer the fourth section.

I (Theresa) obtained a traditional masters degree in counseling psychology and have worked for 14 years in the counseling field with adolescents, families and substance abuse clients. Then I was fortunate enough to find Charles and Nin Bebeau at the Avalon Archetypal Institute in Boulder, Colorado. The Avalon Archetypal Institute offers a two- year certification in Jungian Archetypal Psychotherapy.

Carl Jung (1875-1961) was a psychiatrist, who developed his theories of the unconscious. He was a contemporary of Sigmund Freud, but later broke off the relationship with Freud as he developed his own theories of personality and Soul Psychology. Charles Bebeau Ph. D. studied and read Carl Jung extensively. Dr. Bebeau developed a theory that he believes exemplifies Jung's message to 21st century humanity as we enter the Aquarian Age. Dr. Bebeau developed four stages of alchemical processes whereby we individuate; develop into our potentialities. He also developed the twelve archetypes described in this book and their application to psychotherapy. He has practiced and taught psychotherapy for over thirty years, using this philosophy and techniques.

I have implemented this philosophy and techniques into my private practice and watched it blossom and grow as many clients have reaped the benefits of this wisdom. I find that Dr. Bebeau's normalization of our psychic processes and unconditional acceptance does much to heal. Traditional psychotherapy does much to help people gain an understanding of self, but a lot of it comes from a pathological basis (what's wrong with us, rather than what's right with us), and often tries to suppress these natural cycles of emotion that we all go through. We all naturally have some periods of depression and elation. It is within these natural cycles that our learning, healing, and individuation take place.

This book is my attempt to put this wisdom in the simplest terms possible so that lay people and therapists alike may gain a basic understanding of this theory and perhaps want to pursue it further. This book is meant as an overview and introduction of Soul Psychology as developed by Jung and Bebeau.

Part I

Jungian Archetypal Psychology: Process of the Soul

Carl Jung believed that modern humanity suffers from a disconnection from Soul. He said, "That is because most people find it quite beyond them to live on close terms with the unconscious." [1] He defines unconscious as the aspect of the personality that is hidden from the conscious, waking mind. Dreams, fantasies, hidden desires and agendas belong to the unconscious realm. Jolande Jacobi says, "The ability or inability, rooted in the psyche structure of the individual, to find access to symbols, is one of the reasons Jung's method of deciphering dreams according to their symbolic content is difficult for many to follow. For too many individuals are cut off from the figurative language of their psyche, and these are precisely the highly civilized, the intellectuals. They no longer are capable of grasping anything more than the outward façade, the semiotic aspect of symbol" [2]

Not only are we disconnected from our unconscious; we are also basically disconnected from our bodies, our sexuality, and the Earth. The majority of humanity lives in cities where we walk on concrete. Our air, water, and land are becoming increasingly polluted. We have lost the ability to be intimately attuned to the cycles of Earth, the rising and setting of the Sun, the changing of the seasons in the manner that our ancestors acknowledged it. Their survival was based on an intimate connection with Earth in order to produce food, shelter, clothing, and to nurture their psyches.

Our ancestors were aware that they were somehow connected to the cycles of the universe and so sought to understand this in order to understand themselves. They used astrology for mapping the stars and the effects on the human psyche. The ancient Hebrews predicted the coming of the Christ child ages before hand using their knowledge of the stars. For them, the conjunction of Saturn and Jupiter in a certain pattern, portended a new age and a new messiah [3] Stonehenge and many of the pyramids were placed in such a manner that created alignments with the equinoxes, the solstices, the rising and setting of planets and the moon.

Throughout history, different philosophical and religious systems have separated the mind from the body. The idea is that there is a "better world beyond this one". Some traditions encouraged the neglect of the body by not feeding or bathing it. The most extreme form would be the suicide bomber, giving up one's life in hopes of a better life beyond. Indigenous people realized the connection between the body, mind and spirit and recognized the importance of treating every aspect for optimum health. Today's Holistic Health movement is attempting to bring together these aspects and treat the whole person. Also preventive medicine recognizes the benefits of exercise, nutrition, and the appropriate expression of anger and all emotions for optimum health and in reducing the risk of high blood pressure.

The innovative body worker, Arnold Mindell says,

The biggest problem I encounter is that people have not learned how to work with their feelings. One in a million mothers or fathers say to their children, 'Tell me, how are you feeling in your stomach, in your legs, in your joints? Tell me about your headache. On the contrary, our whole culture is against feeling too much pain. People have still not learned to love themselves, and they have to learn it, they must make a different relationship with themselves towards their bodies. There is no way around it. It's important to accept pain, to sit with it and feel it. [4]

We need to get in the habit of assessing our thoughts, emotions, and physical sensations on a daily basis for optimum health and teaching this to our children.

This is part of preventive medicine, both physical and mental.

[1] C. G. Jung, *Memories, Dreams and Reflections* (New York: Random House, p.228.)

[2] Jolande Jacobi, *Complex/Archetype/Symbol in the Psychology of C.G. Jung* (New York, N.Y.: Princeton University Press, 1959), pp. 87- 88).

[3] Rabbi Joel C. Dobin, D. D., *Kabbalistic Astrology: The Sacred Traditions of the Hebrew Sages* (Rochester, Vt.: Inner Traditions, 1999).

Our relationship to sexuality is also distorted, all the way from religions that suppress sexuality to the commercialization of sexuality. We use sex to sell all sorts of products from soaps to cars. We have a distorted and unhealthy attitude toward the body. We are presented with anorexic models. Some girls and women aspire to look like this, risking their health and very lives to be in vogue.

Women throughout history have been perceived as carrying sexuality, and at times seen as evil for this. It was believed that this was the work of the devil, the sexuality of women distracted men from spiritual matters. Notice the story of Eve, who leads Adam astray by succumbing to the temptation of the serpent, the burning of the "witches" in the Middle Ages for consorting with the devil.[5] This attitude persists even today in parts of the world, where women are required to be covered from head to toe with clothing and are punished if any skin shows. In some countries, women are still stoned to death for adultery. This is reminiscent of Jewish and Christian attitudes in Biblical times.

I think it is appropriate to examine our beliefs and traditions from a more modern egalitarian lens to determine if these customs still apply today. Our concept of equality in the West has grown dramatically over the past forty years; certainly the United States has a history of human rights abuses. The sixties saw the Black movement, the Native American movement, Women's liberation, and more of an appreciation of Eastern religion and thought. The sixties helped to break us out of our old mold.

Even with all the advances we have made, we still need to examine our unconscious stereotypes. Racial profiling still exists. We look at life through a patriarchal (male oriented) lens even yet. We value linear thinking as in math and science over more abstract, creative thinking. We still think it is weak to cry in certain places or certain situations. We don't give equal consideration to emotional expression. Perhaps it is time to take the best of the Old World and combine it with the best of the Modern World.

Although we often consider them primitive from our technological viewpoint, indigenous people had an understanding of the psyche that we have virtually lost contact with. They had little or no criminal activity that we experience today: alcohol/drug addiction, incest, rape, murder, domestic violence, assault, etc. There was more of an appreciation of each individual for what he or she brought to the tribe or society. There was more equality between men and women, children were cherished, homosexuals accepted, and the "mentally ill" looked upon as gifted individuals.

There is a story in the Cheyenne tribe of a chief who suggested a plan to the U. S. government for becoming better aquainted with each other's cultures. He suggested that 12 White women be sent to the tribe to live with them. The government sent 12 women from the mental institution to become part of the tribe. The Native Americans treated all people as special and unique. It is presumed that the women fared better in the Cheyenne tribe than in the insane asylum, where treatment was primitive and inhumane at best.[6]

We have been taught to ignore our dreams, our inner life, and our unconscious minds and to even fear them. There is a belief that we will go "crazy" if we go into our own inner processes too much. Yet connecting to our dreams, our inner life, our unconscious minds, our bodies, our sexuality in a healthy, honoring way, and to the Earth are all ways we connect to our Soul.[7]

In today's society the rational conscious mind is valued over the unconscious. In our school system we are much more likely to fund math and science rather than art, physical education or even self esteem-building curriculum. Is it any wonder so many of our youth are over weight and have a poor self--concept? We spend a great deal of money testing students to see if they have learned the basics, but very little on different models that might facilitate learning for all students.

There is research suggesting that some people learn more visually, others through auditory input, and others through bodily -kinesthetic experiences. For the child who learns through kinesthetic awareness, sitting still for long periods of time is difficult. This child will learn more if she or he can move during the learning process. Also hands –on experience will be more beneficial.

[4]Arnold Mindell, *Working with the Dreaming Body* (London and New York: Routledge and Kegan Paul 1985), p.33.
[5]Riane Eisler, *The Chalice and the Blade* (*San* Francisco: Harper 1995).
[6]Doris Kruse in lecture on Native Americans: Treating Substance Abuse Issues, October 2001.

An old Lakota saying suggests: "Tell me and I'll listen. Show me and I'll understand. Involve me and I'll learn."

> Jung believed that the unconscious was an important part of the psyche. Despite the unlimited extent of its bases, the ego is never more and never less than consciousness as a whole. As a conscious factor the ego could, theoretically at least, be described completely. But this would never amount to more than a picture of the conscious personality; all those features, which are unknown, or unconscious to the subject would be missing. A total picture would have to include these. But a total description of the personality, even in theory, is absolutely impossible, because the unconscious portion of it cannot be grasped cognitively. This unconscious portion, as experience has abundantly shown, is by no means unimportant. On the contrary, the most decisive qualities in a person are often unconscious and can be perceived only by others or have to be laboriously discovered with outside help.[8]

Most of us have had the experience of trying to do something we don't really want to do. It is difficult for our conscious mind to talk us into doing something our unconscious mind really doesn't ascribe to. An example would be: In my Soul I am really an artist, but society and my rational mind believes that I can't make a living with my art, so I deny the artist part of myself. I will always be in conflict with myself. I may even do something to sabotage myself, like not show up for my day job so that I intentionally get fired. I have created chaos in my life. I need money to live on, but I acknowledge that the job really didn't fulfill me. Maybe somewhere in the confusion I will develop a plan for fulfilling my Soul's desires and for earning a living. Maybe I will find work that is more creative or promise myself that when I have earned a certain amount of money, I will give myself time to do what I really enjoy. It is important to honor the unconscious part of the psyche, in order to become a more whole, functioning, individualized person. To not do so would be like using half of one's employees in completing a project. One half of the staff would do all the work and the other half may resent it and not feel valued.

The alchemical process is a model for working with the Soul's evolution. In this model there is the belief that the Soul is not some static entity, but that we ourselves are constantly changing, growing, and learning.

[7] Charles Bebeau, Ph. D. lecture in Praxis III, spring 2001.

[8] C.G. Jung, *Aion: Researches into the Phenomenology of the Self* (New York, N.Y.: Princeton University Press, 1968) p. 5.

Alchemical Process

Alchemists of Medieval times combined studies of the Hebrew Qabbala and Greek philosophy to create alchemy, a science to aid humans in developing their individual potential. The alchemists used an analogy of turning lead into gold to describe the process of the evolution of the soul.

Jung studied alchemy and astrology along with different cultures of the world. Many cultures of the world believe that our souls are androgynous, containing aspects of both masculine and feminine. This was also reflected in their portrayal of divinity, having both gods and goddesses. Hinduism and Chinese Taoism are examples of this concept. Susanne Schaup in her book Sophia says,

> The principle of Taoism is illustrated by the well-known symbol of two intertwined halves, a light and a dark one, contained within a circle. At the point of the greatest expansion of one part, the other germinally appears as a tiny spot. The symbol represents the perfect balance of Yin and Yang, the central polarities of the Taoist worldview. The light part (Yang) is considered masculine, active and "positive," or Heaven; the dark (Yin) represents the feminine, passive and "negative," or Earth. Originally, there was no judgment or value attached to either "positive" or "negative." These were simply terms to symbolize polarity. This changed with the patriarchal shift, which took place in China as everywhere else in prehistoric times, but the original intuition of equivalent polarities working together in harmony was not affected by it. [9]

Jung also developed the theory that each of us contains masculine and feminine energies within our souls. Men carry an anima, or feminine energy and women an animus, or masculine energy. Our task is to create a divine union or marriage between these energies within ourselves in order to individuate, to become more fully who we really are. Then we, as individuals, are able to use the assertiveness, out in the world energy of the masculine as well as the more in depth, soulful, nurturing aspect of the feminine. In this way we become more self-reliant and we attract healthy individuals into relationship with us. What is inside of us is reflected outside in our world.

The alchemical process is evident in our daily lives through our dreams, our relationships with others, and our awareness of our bodies. In the past giving attention to dreams was discouraged by some religious traditions because dreams often contain sexual content or conflict. It was believed that dreams were evil forces within us, trying to lead us astray. I believe that the Soul wants to show us its process toward individuation, sometimes in a dramatic way. The second area to pay attention to is our relationships. We can notice if we are having conflictual or harmonious relationships with other women or men. The third area is body symptoms. Some area in our body may be directing our attention to it through pain or an unusual sensation. Later in the book, archetypes will be described. Each. Archetype relates to an area of the body. We get a clue as to which archetype we are working with by noticing the area of the body emphasized in the dream.

The Soul also has a natural cycle of descents and integration it goes through, what we would normally term as depression and perhaps mania. Part of our task is to recognize and be comfortable with these cycles in our lives. They are part of our personal growth process.

Charles Bebeau, Ph.D. has expanded on Jung's work and developed the four levels of alchemical process. The four levels are divided into two phases. Although this explanation describes dream images, it also relates to our waking life—body symptoms and relationships. An explanation of this alchemical process follows. There are also two charts that follow the alchemical section that further describe dream images and the alchemical Soul Process. [10]

---

[9] Susanne Schaup, *Sophia* (York Beach: Nicolas-Hays, Inc. 1997), p.188-89.

[10] Charles Bebeau Ph.D., lecture Praxis II Autumn 2000,also see 2 charts that further describe alchemical stages.

Phase I

This phase relates to dream images of the individual dreamer or images of the same gender as the dreamer. They relate to the ego/body. As understood in Holistic Health, the ego and the body are connected. Our appearance very much affects how we see ourselves, how we present ourselves. Many times a particular lifestyle leads to specific body symptoms; such as a Type A personality may develop high blood pressure. This philosophy isn't meant to blame us for our illness, but to help us be aware of the mind/body connection and how it relates to archetypes. The purpose of Phase I processes is to develop a strong ego to support the Soul.

Level 1 dream imagery is characterized by conflict, death of the old ego structure. "In this work **Shadow** refers to an archetypal aspect that an individual carries that is not fully developed, integrated, or expressed." It can also be an aspect that is overdone, such as anger in a warrior or a preoccupation with war. "When painful experiences, unacceptable desires or images are repressed, they move to the unconscious, "where they emerge later in a way that is wounded".[11] Shadow materials are negatively valued aspects of ourselves that we often don't see or want to acknowledge in ourselves. We often project them on to other people. For example, we may think we don't get angry when we really do. Instead of acknowledging that anger, we accuse our partner of always being angry. It is often easier to see both good and negative traits in someone else rather than in oneself.

This is a descent phase where negatively valued aspects of oneself are brought to awareness. There is awareness that one must change at a deep level. Life has become meaningless. This phase is often marked by depression. It could be called the Dark Night of the Soul. (See chart following this section for dream images of all levels.) Imagine a bouquet of four roses: one black, one white, one yellow, and one red. This represents the alchemical process. The color black characterizes this level. It is the black rose.

Level 2 is integration within oneself, a new creation of an ego structure. Dream images would include the wholeness or healing of the body. Sometimes there are dream images of sex with the same gender. This does not imply that the dreamer is necessarily homosexual. This is the Soul's image of integration of the ego/body. The white rose characterizes this level.

Phase II

This stage relates to dream images of the opposite gender. A man's inner Soul is his Anima. A woman's inner Soul is her Animus. In this stage there is awareness of shadow material regarding the contra-sexual anima/animus and an integration of these elements into the conscious Self.

Level 3 involves conflict with the opposite gender. Dream images include chase, rape, death, disease, or dismemberment. The yellow rose characterizes this level.

Level 4 is integration of the contra-sexual self into the whole Self. Dream images include intimate union with the opposite gender. The red rose characterizes this level.

---

[11] Patricia Keeler *Incest: Quest for Soul Union, 2001*, (unpublished Ph. D dissertation).

Ego/Body Tyme Line of transmutation	Albedo Ascent into Ego/Body Union &Identity	Deep Soul Tyme	Ruebedo Ascent into Soul/Self Reunion
Negredo Descent into Ego/Body Shadow Material		Xanthosis Descent into Anima/ Animus conflict	

Tyme Division Line

Alchemical Stages

Albedo Phase I Ego/Body This phase is concerned with the further development of the ego identity and sense of self. Making conscious the personal shadow and integrating it into the Self. The death and resurrection of the Ego/Body. Dreams in this phase are characterized by same-sex images.		Ruebedo Phase II Deep Soul This phase is concerned with making conscious the inner contra-sexual shadow and integrating those elements (Anima/Animus) into the conscious Self. The death and resurrection of the Soul. Dreams in this phase are characterized by opposite-sex images.	
1. Negredo	**2. Albedo**	**3.Citrinitis**	**4. Ruebedo**

The Black Rose
    This sub phase marks the death of the old ego structure. A conflicted stage, it is a descent process on a personal level where there is a coming to awareness of the negatively valued aspects of our own nature. This phase also is marked by depression, the realization that one is living a lie, the life is meaningless, an examination of ones mode of life, that one must change at a deep inner level and shed obsolete aspects of self. It can be called "The Dark Night of the Soul."
 	
    Dream Images: Chaos, destruction, death, disease, dismemberment, or conflict imagery concerning self or a member of the same sex, always negatively toned. Wild animals, especially dogs, representing un-integrated body/ego issues. These animals generally manifest according to archetypal themes. The front porch or façade of a house, the basement, a wild
	The White Rose
	    This sub phase marks the creation of a new ego structure, a new relationship with oneself with greater integration and wholeness. It is a coming to terms with our sense of self and our own sex and gender identity. It is marked by a new feeling of wholeness in oneself, a rebirth or transformation of Self; the greater integration of shadow material into the Self and is an indicator of healing, the ego purified with obsolete issues and wounds shed.
	
	Dream Images: The body healed or transformed, positive imagery concerning self or a same sex character, possibly sexual imagery pertaining to a member of the same sex or verbal innuendo. Rebuilding or renovation of the façade or front porch of a house , building a new foundation on the old. Also positive interaction with animals, again according to the archetype in question.
		The Yellow Rose
		    This sub phase, also called Xanthosis, was dropped
		    from the system when Alchemy was Christianized. It is perhaps the most important one in pursuing the opus. It is the stage of confronting ones internal contra-sexual shadow material and marks the need to establish a new relationship with ones' Anima/Animus.
		
		Dream Images: Chase, rape, death, disease, dismemberment, or conflict imagery, possibly subtle, concerning a member of the opposite sex. Strong projection of inner issues onto members of the opposite sex—that they can do nothing good or right or that they're at "fault". Other images can concern the "upstairs" of a house, particularly if the image has negative connotations. Generally unpleasant imagery pertaining to the opposite sex. Divorce or the ending of an opposite sex relationship is common during this phase.
			The Red Rose
			    This sub phase marks the rebirth of the soul, the greater integration of the contra-sexual self into wholeness with the Self. The transformation of the Shadow wounds exposed in the Citrinitis (#3) sub phase; the Heirosgamos or sacred marriage.
			
			Dream Images: Intimate union with the opposite sex, positive imagery concerning a member of the opposite sex, sexual dreams, kissing, sitting on a bed or in intimate circumstances, dancing, marriage (esp. 2 couples being married or being erotic together). Mandala imagery, circles and circular figure, squared, 4 of anything, possibly dreams of conception and/or birth (the divine child). The child born will be of the opposite sex. Women generally have more detailed birth imagery and nurturing imagery. Men can also experience birth or pregnancy imagery, but usually not in the detail of women. Sometimes the child will be ill and need to be nurtured to full health.

backyard or wilderness representing uncontrolled/ unacknowledged aspects of Self.			

Archetypes

Archetypes are universal patterns of energy that manifest in the human psyche. They are "pre-existent to consciousness" …and "therefore cannot be considered an invention of consciousness." [12] If we examine the myths and literature of the world, we can identify certain images that are evident across all cultures. These images are also living in individuals today. Following is a description of the 12 archetypes developed and characterized by Charles Bebeau, Ph.D. He believes that these archetypes live within each of us and that specifically we will each embody 4, 5, or 6 of these archetypes in our own unique way. It gives each of us our own unique personality, our likes, dislikes, and even determines the kind of people we are attracted to. I believe that it can help us cultivate more tolerance for each other as individuals. It explains why each of us is a unique person, unlike anyone else.

Following this introduction is a scenario I created so that the 12 archetypes could come to life and be more easily recognizable within each of us. In the description of the cast (which are the archetypes), I have identified the manner in which these archetypes would appear in therapy and issues associated with each archetype. I have also traced the way I imagine these archetypes would appear in early humanity and the way they have been wounded in modern society and perhaps some attitudes and techniques we can use to heal these archetypes in ourselves and in society as a whole. For in healing ourselves and bringing ourselves into right perspective, we heal our families, society, and ultimately the planet. It would be interesting to recognize the archetypes in yourself as you read the descriptions.

Six of the archetypes are represented as masculine and six as feminine, but they appear in men and women equally. They may also appear as the opposite gender in our dreams, depending on the stage of the dream. For example: I may have a dream of myself riding a horse. This would be represented by the teacher/traveler archetype, which is a male energy. But I am female, so a male energy appears in a female body. Or a man may dream of himself as a chef, representing the Nourishing Mother, obviously a feminine energy, but appearing in a male body.

The ancient people envisioned the constellations in the sky to be a cosmic human, with each sign representing a part of the body, starting with the head in Aries and ending with the feet in Pisces. Each archetype is also related to a particular area of the body. A person carrying this archetype may have an emphasis or exaggeration in that part of the body. This is not to say that we create our illnesses, but that the archetype may be expressed through that area of the body. The body is the vessel; it tells you what the Soul is doing. It's a spiritual process. (See the body chart on the next page for the area of body represented by each archetype.)

The number twelve has been of importance throughout history. The Romans and Greeks identified a pantheon of 12: 6 gods and 6 goddesses. Ancient people identified 12 constellations. Astrology is the oldest science. The ancient Hebrews were astrologers and as mentioned before, they prophesized the coming of Jesus for centuries by identifying patterns in the stars.

---

[12] *Memories, Dreams, Reflections,* p. 348.

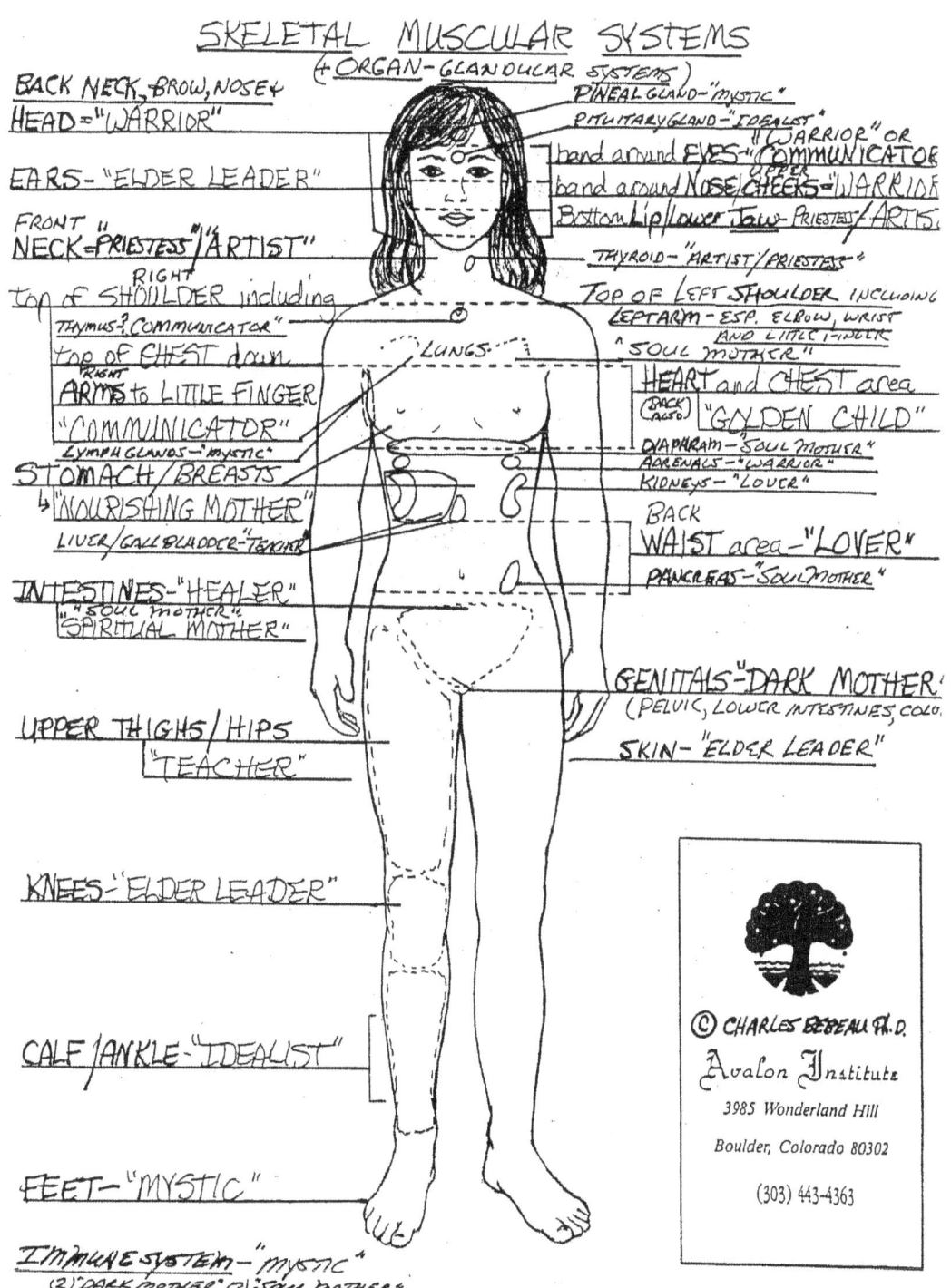

Areas of the body related to the Archetypes

Part II

The cast of characters known as The Twelve Archetypes
With illustrations by Sarah Trumpp

THE WARRIOR - "LANCELOT"

Warrior (Lancelot)

Ruled by Mars in Aries, it is the beginning of spring. It is a cardinal (beginning), fire, male sign. The god Ares represents this archetype.

Area of body affiliated with this archetype: the head, as in the helmet area, the temples, neck, sinus, and the cardiovascular and adrenal system

History of archetype: In a healthy manner the warrior protects a society from intrusion. He patrols the boundaries. But throughout history, the warrior has conquered more peaceful, less fortified societies. This dominator legacy has continued through today, although there is more awareness of human rights for all.

Mission Statement: To Pioneer change.

Characteristics: Aries is the cardinal sign of spring. It is the initiator, and so it begins the description of the archetypes. The Warrior is about the expression of personal power, life direction. It represents one's personality, identity, how we present to the world. The warrior enjoys being very active physically; at times he can push his/her body too hard and so is accident-prone. S/he would be involved in activities such as running, bicycling, and sports. He would likely be active all his life and concerned about his/her physical appearance, as well as want his/her mate to be attractive.

The Warrior's mission is to pioneer change, to right the wrongs in the world. He is the physical energy behind a project. He is the entrepreneur, but sometimes has difficulty staying with a project once he has started it. He usually needs one of the other archetypes within his psyche to be the brains behind a project, to choose which mission to champion and to provide the staying power.

The Warrior is fiery in nature and quick to anger, but also quick to express it. Sometimes he impulsively blurts out his thoughts without thinking it through and others feel hurt by his words. Just as quickly he moves on. There is a naïve quality about him. We always invite the energy we put out in the world. Since his mode is to be impulsive, at times to attack, he is often also attacked. The Warrior is quick-witted, competitive. He likes speed. He can physically do 4-5 things at a time. S/he is adventurous and often a risk-taker.

Women who embody this energy sometimes have a difficult time connecting to their personal power and expressing their anger. They were taught that girls don't get angry. It is important to translate anger into personal power and direction in one's life. Women sometimes also have difficulty being physically active. Again it isn't always supported by the culture.

Therapeutic Issues: He will often show up in therapy in connection with charges of road rage, assault, and domestic violence. He needs to learn appropriate ways to manage his anger. As mentioned before, women may need support and encouragement to connect to their personal power, to express their anger, to be comfortable with being physically active or playing sports. .

This archetype will also often show up in combination with the Mystic in the DUI (driving under the influence of drugs and alcohol) population. Most states require that DUI offenders complete some type of education and therapy to address their drunk driving behavior. This is often coupled with other sanctions from the state including losing the driver's license and taking antabuse, which makes the individual ill if s/he consumes alcohol. Physical exercise is important to the warrior to channel some of his/her abundant energy. Deep breathing exercises would also help him/her to relax.

Dream Images: hawks, cars, bicycles, guns, knives, and all types of weapons.

ARTIST ~ PRIESTESS
"INANNA"

Artist/Priestess (Inanna)

Ruled by Venus in Taurus, which is the middle of spring. It is a fixed, Earth feminine sign.

Area of body affiliated with this archetype: the throat, tongue, and lower jaw.

History of archetype: Inanna was a Sumerian (now Iraq) Goddess. She reigned until approximately 3500 B.C.E. She had many great temples which served as educational centers, specializing in the arts and sciences and in which artist/priestesses spent their days creating art. These women were skilled at all kinds of arts: painting, pottery, singing, dancing, and theatre. The temples were also Spiritual and healing centers. Sexuality was used as a teaching and therapeutic tool Men would go there to learn the art of lovemaking, or improve their technique. Marduk (a Sumerian warrior) conquered the Mother cultures. The temples were defiled, the women declared prostitutes. (For more information on this topic, please see The Chalice and the Blade by Riane Eisler.) Other goddesses representing this energy are Isis, the Egyptian Queen, and Astarte of the Hebrew tradition.

Mission Statement: To beautify the world, take spirit and give it form.

Characteristics: People who embody this archetype are born with an innate desire to create beauty in the world. They have an eye for color, texture, form and composition. Every project is a creative expression, whether it is decorating a room, creating a garden, or designing clothing. Men who embody this archetype are often employed in housing construction and in fine wood- working. Native Americans and people of African descent embody this archetype with their artistic creations. Many indigenous cultures incorporated art into their lifestyle, unlike modern culture, which doesn't put much value on artistic endeavor and where artists often struggle for years for recognition and any sort of income.

The Artist/Priestess is very sensuous and loves beautiful things, including jewelry. She gathers information through the senses: touch, smell, taste, and auditory. This energy rules the voice: using vibration in the throat to communicate and sing. It is important to speak his/her truth. To hold back, s/he risks unleashing all the pent up anger at once in a torrent of rage and then later regretting what s/he said. She also risk's holding onto a grudge if s/he doesn't express herself .She likes demonstrations of physical affection and can be rather demanding when she doesn't get it.

Because it is a fixed Earth sign she takes longer processing information than some of the other archetypes, such as the Communicator. Because of this, the artist may doubt his/her intelligence, but she just processes information at a deeper level than others. She will also resist any prodding, which conflicts with her will, but she is loyal and determined.

People carrying this energy are very erotic and just naturally attract the attention of others. Her partner may think she is doing something to attract this attention, when she just naturally carries this erotic energy. People will notice it in her, without her doing anything. .

She sometimes has doubts about her own sexuality and physical attraction. Many of the feminine energies carry a wound concerning the body, especially the feminine body and anything concerning sex. For many centuries, and even today in certain religions, the Spiritual realm is considered more ideal than being in an earthly body and women are expected to cover all parts of the body, except for the eyes. Sexual favors are only to be given to the husband, who basically has ownership of the woman. The Artist/ Priestess went from celebrating the sexuality of her body in a healthy manner to being called a temple prostitute.

She often times will have full lips, a full round face, a husky, sensuous voice. Since it is an oral energy and she has a sweet tooth, she may have difficulty with managing her weight. She is a healer in a physical, practical sense. She makes an excellent body worker, such as a massage therapist.

Therapeutic Issues: The artist must do his/her art. And speak one's truth. We often call this archetype, along with the Soul Mother, the give away women. She tends to give herself away in relationships and think it is her fault if there is problems in the relationship, resulting in self esteem issues. In therapy we are going to do some education around the wounds incurred in this archetype to help her realize "it's not her fault" and to help her develop an appreciation of her talents and increase self-esteem.

Dream Images: bull, buffalo, gorilla, monkey, deer, gems, things of beauty.

COMMUNICATOR
"MERCURIOUS"

Communicator (Mercurious)

Ruled by Mercury in Gemini. It is a mutable (changing), male air sign. Air represents mental energy.

Area of body affiliated with this archetype: Gemini rules the right lung, top of the right shoulder, arm, hand, and small finger. There is an electrical energy that pulsates from his eyes.

History of archetype: In the Sumerian legend, Mercury (or Mummu as he was called by the Sumerians) was the first planet created by Apsu (Sun) and Tiamat (the precursor of Earth). Mummu had an erratic, wobbly orbit, traveling between Apsu and Tiamat. He was therefore considered a messenger of the Gods. This description of Mercury (Hermes) continued into the Roman and Greek traditions, where he was also considered the messenger of Jupiter (Zeus). In the oral traditions of old, stories and information was passed from generation to generation orally. The great orators in the Native American traditions would exemplify this.

Mission Statement: To link, connect highest with deepest; become the messenger. They get high on words and will use words to guide them through life.

Characteristics: This is a rather young, androgynous energy. S/he is articulate, rules all types of communication: writing, speaking, broadcasting, etc. S/he enjoys linking with other minds and connecting ideas. He is at home in the information age. He is glib and always has a pat answer. Computers and advanced technology are his arenas, especially the telephone, as that is the quickest way to communicate. (Uranus also rules the computer and the Internet.) He is very quick-witted, logical, compiles and disseminates information. He is valued in our quick, technological society. He talks rapidly, and uses his hands to emphasis his message. (He is ruled by Mercury, after all.) S/he can carry on several conversations or read several books at one time. At times he is rather anxious and can have a lot of critical head chatter. Communicator children do well in our school system because they process information quickly, ask many questions, especially "why?" Sometimes that becomes a little taxing to adults around them. Communicators are good at using their hands, working with a computer. The Communicator also overlaps into the Artist/ Priestess area, as s/he is good at instruments requiring fingering such as the piano, guitar, flute, etc. Gemini also rules short trips, say within one's own country or state.

Therapeutic Issues: Sometimes s/he is very anxious because of all the nervous energy. S/he also may have issues around the use of nicotine, caffeine, and amphetamines. He may use alcohol to dull the critical chatter in his mind, so it will be important to address addictive issues in therapy. Using his/her hands in a project or working with a computer will channel some of the nervous energy, along with exercise and deep breathing exercises. Meditation also helps calm the mind.

Dream Images: different forms of communication: speaking writing: windows, cameras, lens, and the eyes.

NOURISHING MOTHER
"MAMA"

Nourishing Mother (Mama)

Ruled by the moon in Cancer. It is a cardinal, feminine water sign. It begins summer. The moon is considered reflective because it reflects the light of the Sun

Area of body affiliated with this archetype: The breasts and the stomach.

History of archetype: Throughout patriarchal history, this has been the most accepted role for women: homemaker, wife, and mother, providing sustenance for the family. Nourishing Mother is one aspect of the Great Mother Goddess in pre-patriarchal society. She is the all-giving nourishing part of the Goddess; feeding all her children on Earth; from her abundant body. The Willendorf Goddess (unearthed near Willendorf, Austria, which is approximately 30,000 years old) is representative of this archetype. The Willendorf Goddess has large, enormous breasts and stomach, from which all of creation emerged. The ancient people gave much importance to the feminine aspect of creation. They saw that women became pregnant and that life emerged from their womb and babies were nourished at their breasts.

Mission Statement: Building home, deep connection to family, community, and ones ancestral background.

Characteristics: She likes building home, to cook, serve others, mother her children. She has endless patience and usually is able to serve others without losing herself. She often feels frustrated when she can't mother children or pets (which are like children). She is very emotional, sensitive, and comfortable in expressing these emotions, in fact you will know when she has been hurt or unappreciated for the service she gives others. She seems to have an intuitive body sense; she knows with her body. S/he makes a good chef. She has great organizational ability.

This is a difficult energy for men to carry as it is so sensitive, but when men can accept the nurturing, sensitive part of themselves, it becomes easier. In fact it really is a personal strength to be able to give to others. This archetype can appear rather shy.

Therapeutic Issues: With the Women's liberation movement, women who stay home with their children may not feel valued by society. In therapy, we are going to help the Nourishing Mother feel good about self and the role s/he plays in the family and society. Sometimes she doesn't feel appreciated, that whatever recognition s/he receives is not enough. Inner child work would be helpful in this instance, to help her mother herself. Also since this archetype can be shy, some assertiveness training is helpful.

Dream Images: breasts, stomach, food, Mother, home.

"ARTHUR"
THE GOLDEN CHILD

Golden Child (Arthur)

Ruled by the Sun in Leo. It is a fixed, male fire sign. (What is more fiery than the Sun.) This is the middle of summer. The Sun represents Soul Mission, which could be described as the best example of what a human can create.

Area of body affiliated with this archetype: heart, the upper back. There is a heart full connection with others. The heart pumps lifeblood throughout the whole body and therefore is a big determinate of our health and vitality, the energy we put into life.

History of archetype: This is the King. The Christ Child represents this energy, with the interplay of humanity and divinity. Jesus had a soul mission while he was here on Earth: to bring forth his message of love and compassion. Another historical figure representing this archetype would be King Arthur; very diplomatic, charismatic, and much loved by his followers. The chief of a Native American tribe, who often lead by consensus, would represent the diplomacy and democracy of this archetype.

Mission Statement: Creative Leadership. Bill Clinton with his Leo Sun and George W. Bush with Leo rising are examples of creative leadership. They have become world leaders in trying to bring better living conditions to all the people in the world, not just America.

Characteristics: As the Sun illuminates the sky and the planets reflect back this light, the Golden Child wants to create an environment that reflects him or her, whether it is a biological creation as in a child or a creative work of art. The Golden Child is a very fertile, fiery energy. It produces children, which is also a reflection or creation of ourselves.

S/he is Charismatic, generous, enthusiastic, confidant, and a natural-born leader. He models courage and integrity to those around him. S/he will often create his or her kingdom/queendom around himself/herself. He finds himself called upon to represent his culture or community. Capricorn or Elder Leader energy also deals with leadership, but it is more of a cultural leadership, there is an ethnic quality to it. Golden Child is more general, less specific. It doesn't particularly care what kind of leader s/he is. He just naturally leads the people who are gathered around him with his enthusiasm and Charisma. Elder Leader is more structured and sometimes domineering, especially in it's wounded aspect. The Golden Child would lead in a more charismatic manner.

S/he is generous, but feels wounded if s/he is not appreciated. Sometimes they will rely on their charisma to get them by in life. S/he is also subject to flattery. Sometimes other people are resentful of his self-confidence and apparent lack of faults. The spouse of someone with Golden Child can't be too possessive, as this energy is very sexy, charismatic and will attract other people. To the Golden Child, life is playful, simple, and innocent. Many Actors/actresses and politicians have Golden Child dominate in their charts.

Therapeutic Issues: Relationship issues would bring this archetype into therapy. It is possible that s/he would come into therapy if other people projected their envy on him and then deflated him when the projection was removed injuring his/her pride.

Dream Images: lion, big cats, the sun, and the king. This would indicate Golden child energy within oneself.

SOUL MOTHER
"SOPHIA"

Soul Mother (Sophia)

Ruled by Mercury in Virgo (Mercury also rules Gemini). This sign is the transition point between summer and autumn. It is a mutable, feminine Earth sign.

Area of body affiliated with this archetype: The digestive system, left lung, top left shoulder, and arm, down to the little finger. This archetype also rules the immune system (along with the Dark Mother and Mystic).

History of archetype: Sumer is believed to be the oldest civilization on Earth. It is located in Mesopotamia in modern day Iraq. Sumerian legend speaks of Tiamat (maiden of life) from whom the other planets were created. [13] In the beginning, there was Apsu (the Sun) and Tiamat. The waters (primordial elements) of Apsu and Tiamat commingled and produced the other planets. Later the 12th Planet or Nibiru (Marduk in the Babylonian legend) rammed into Tiamat and cleaved her. The Earth was also called Ki (the cleaved one) in ancient legends. Part of Tiamat became the Earth and part became the "hammered bracelet" or the asteroid belt between Mars and Jupiter.

Mission Statement: Strong healing service. She is the soulful feminine.

Characteristics: She is very connected to the Earth, nature, plants and animals (dogs, cats, birds, and flying insects are connected to this archetype). Loves humanity and being in service to them. Soul Mothers make good therapists, nutritionists, and herbalists. Soul Mothers are also very physically creative in arts such as weaving, sewing and musical expression.

There is a belief system that the Bible is rooted in older myths and the history of ancient peoples. Ninhursag was the Sumerian Queen who, along with her brother Ea, developed humanity. She would be representative of the Soul Mother energy. This archetype is represented as Wisdom in the Old Testament, but she gradually becomes a concept rather than an entity as she is gradually written out of the Bible. Divine Wisdom is the co-creator of the universe. She is the divine feminine figure and Yahweh's playmate.

> Then I was at his side each day,
> His darling and delight,
> Playing in his presence continually. (Proverbs 8:30) [14]

She is known as Sophia in the Greek tradition and Chokma in the Jewish tradition. This archetype developed a "Wisdom wound" as she was no longer recognized for her wisdom aspect. Mother Mary is reminiscent of Wisdom in the Old Testament, but without much of the power and wisdom.

She is a deep, soul energy, and because she is connected to the Earth, she usually processes information more slowly than some of the other archetypes. Because of this she often doubts her intelligence, and so may have difficulty in school. Where the communicator child compiles information, Soul Mother possesses a deeper, more philosophical (Sophia comes from this word) wisdom. The Soul Mother will withdraw from society when she doesn't feel appreciated. She will usually return after she has had time to nurture herself and rebuild self-confidence. Solitude and being in nature are key elements to her/his emotional as well as physical health.

This is a very powerful, but also very wounded archetype. People with this archetype sometimes have difficulty being embodied. Throughout patriarchal history and in many religions, the physical body was degraded, considered less desirable and holy than the Spiritual realm; particularly the feminine body and all the functions associated with it. Women were the "seed of the Devil", tempting men into sexuality, diverting their thoughts away from God. Soul Mother archetype carries the deep shame of being in a

---

[13] The 12th Planet, Zecharia Sitchin, Avon Books, Inc., 1976.

[14] For a more comprehensive view of this topic please see Sophia, by Susanne Schaup, Nicolas-Hays, Inc., 1997.

physical body, perhaps because this archetype has continually been demoted time after time. First it was a planet, then a co-creator of God.

The Soul Mother, along with the Dark Mother, has traditionally been a healer. These women and men helped birth babies, and ministered to the sick and dying. During the middle Ages, the Church decided that only male physicians educated at the university were permitted to administer to the sick and wounded. Their knowledge was fairly primitive by today's standards. They often used leaches to bleed people; whereas, the traditional healers were versed in herbology and other arts of healing. These women and some men were often accused of witchcraft and were burned at the stake; their property confiscated. It is estimated that 3 million people (mostly women) were murdered over 3 centuries.[14]

People with this archetype often inherit the wounds as well. This archetype can either be very neat and clean or messy in house keeping habits. Soul Mother can be very ritualistic; there is a certain, prescribed way to perform tasks; such as house cleaning, bathing or sex. Physical experience is part of the Spiritual experience; we must manifest in a physical body in order to develop and evolve in our Soul Process.

The Soul Mother loves humanity and can see the potential in people. Sometimes it becomes a problem when she becomes impatient with the slowness with which people manifest their potential. Also she may focus only on the potential and ignore the reality of the situation.

Therapeutic Issues: Breath work is helpful to Soul Mothers for its calming effect and to develop more healthy breathing habits. We habitually hold our breath when we are stressed, which produces problems with the immune and respiratory system. (Soul Mother rules the respiratory and immune system), so breathe work is especially important to her. The immune system stays healthy when we can introduce plenty of oxygen in our system. Soul Mothers will also suffer from self-esteem issues and is the other give-away girl in relationships, along with the Artist/Priestess, so we will work on those issues in therapy. The mission of the Soul Mother is to bring together body and soul. The original alchemists understood that body and soul were connected, but throughout history, the two became disconnected. The body is the vessel, it tells you what the Soul is doing.

Dream Images: nature, dogs, cats, corn, wheat, owl, birds, and trees.

---

[14] *Women's Spirituality: The Burning Times,* Rocky Mountain Public Broadcasting.

"ROMEO"
LOVER

Lover

Also ruled by Venus in Libra. Lover is a male, air sign. It is a cardinal sign, as it begins autumn.

Area of body affiliated with this archetype: The kidney area, the back of the waist

History of archetype: The Chivalrous knight of the Middle Ages.

Mission Statement: To make relationship transcendent, to create a new form of partnership

Characteristics: Libra is opposite of the Warrior or Aries on the zodiac wheel. Where as Aries seeks personal power, the Lover seeks fulfillment in another.

S/he is interested in intimate relationships with another. There is a drive to relationship, the balance of the Yin and Yang. This is the Spiritual Mission. He sees his lover as a mirror of himself. This energy can become wounded when there is a need to always be in a relationship, or to avoid relationships altogether.

Lovers are diplomatic, seeing both sides of an issue. They make good mediators. They seek balance in all parts of life, even to the point of not speaking up so as to not cause a disturbance. They are good social directors, hosts and hostesses. They love beautiful surroundings and beautiful things.

Today, the quest for a good relationship is almost like the spiritual quest for the Holy Grail or religious experience in the past. It is the path to self-development. It is more common today, to marry for love, where as in the past, many marriages were arranged. We have serial monogamy in the quest to find the "right person" who will fulfill us. Sometimes we avoid working on our own issues and instead think we will find happiness and fulfillment in a different or better relationship. On the other hand, there is more flexibility in relationships; we can marry outside of our ethnic background or choose not to marry at all. Also, there is no longer the pressure to remain in an abusive relationship as there once was.

Therapeutic Issues: The Lover would come into therapy for relationship issues, which is a reason a large percentage of people seek therapy.

Dream Images: love birds, scales, beautiful surroundings, love relationships.

DARK MOTHER
"SABRINA"

Dark Mother (Sabrina)

Ruled by Pluto in Scorpio, she is the queen of the underworld. This is a fixed (middle of autumn), feminine water sign. Again water is deep, emotional. It is opposite Taurus in the zodiac. Both are erotic and sensual.

Area of body affiliated with this archetype: The reproductive area of the body, large intestine. It also rules the immune system (along with Soul Mother and Mystic).

History of archetype: She is the life force. She understands the transitions in life: helping babies come into this life or helping a soul to transition to the other side. In the Mother culture she was the Queen of the Underworld (hence the name Dark Mother), a place where souls went between lives. Ereshkigal exemplifies this archetype in the Sumerian legends. Other representatives of this archetype are Hecate, Kali and Persephone. Lilith and the Black Madonna would represent this energy in the Judeo-Christian tradition. Lilith was believed to be Adam's first wife, but refused "to lie beneath" him as she told him they were created equal. She left him and became vilified as a repulsive hag who seduces men and murders children for her independence and disobedience (See *Sophia* by Susanne Schaup, pp.34-43).

Mission Statement: To honor the deep, passionate part of self.

Characteristics: Dark Mother is transformational energy: life, death, and sexuality. She rules the reproductive area of the body. Dark Mothers make good healers, hospice workers, midwives, and therapists, as they work with the deep, underlying life processes. S/he likes emotional intensity, although at times it is frightening to her as well as to others, feels thwarted if s/he can't express those seething emotions. Our society doesn't usually allow an expression of intense emotions like anger and grief, but if these emotions are held in too long, they will be expressed as rage or depression if we don't work through the grief process.

Dark Mother has been very wounded and maligned through out history. Along with Soul Mother, she was the healer, the midwife, and the one who administered to the dying and was accused of witch -craft in the Middle Ages and burned at the stake.

Dark Mother carries deep, erotic energy and is often feared by others or abused sexually by others who don't honor, respect or even know how to deal appropriately with sexual energy in themselves or others. But to restrict and repress sexual energy creates an obsession and shame around it. People who don't acknowledge their own personal and sexual power are more likely to be attacked by someone wounded in the expression of their own sexuality. Men are afraid of the woman who is really in her power and not afraid to demonstrate that. Of course, we must have boundaries around our sexuality, but also free expression of it.

Therapeutic Issues This is probably the most wounded archetype, given society's issues with sex and death. People with this archetype are going to naturally carry some of those wounds, even with the healthiest upbringing. If there are any sexual abuse issues, those need to be addressed in therapy. Dark Mother can become addicted to the intense emotional experience of cocaine, so those issues would also be addressed in therapy. Pluto stays in one sign for approximately 12 years and so defines a generation. It was in its home sign of Scorpio from 1983-1995. The teens born in that era, exemplify the Dark Mother, with their Gothic look and sometimes their preoccupation with death, suicide, sexuality, and drug abuse. Education about the Dark Mother is helpful in bringing about understanding and raising one's self-esteem.

Dream Images: scorpion, snake, eagle, reptiles, were–wolves, mud, muck, feces.

TEACHER/TRAVELER
"PROFESSOR"

Teacher/Traveler (Professor)

Ruled by Jupiter in Sagittarius. It is a mutable, male fire sign, the transition between autumn and winter.

Area of body affiliated with this archetype: The buttocks and thighs.

History of archetype: The Spiritual teacher, philosopher, the guru, Zeus, Jupiter. This is the Spiritual Father.

Mission Statement: To synthesize principles to the highest meaning.

Characteristics: The teacher/traveler is an adventurous sort of person who likes to learn about other cultures by traveling there, or at least studying them. As the name suggests, they are also teachers, publishers, lawyers, philosophers, working with their own and other people's belief systems. This makes them good therapists, as the work of therapy is often about changing the way we perceive a situation.

This is the teacher, the Guru, the Spiritual teacher. Teacher types will generate a following around them. They want to help their students grow in a profound way; to challenge them to think creatively. Teachers get energized by teaching others, but hate to be interrupted because they have an agenda, certain areas of information they want to impart to others.

Teacher/Travelers like to learn; sometimes they are career students. They prefer experiential learning to memorization of facts. Sometimes this causes problems with the educational system and they may leave a group or an educational situation in an angry manner and perhaps find a group that meets their needs or begin one of their own. Often they will drop out of school and travel to get their education. The Soul Mother also has difficulty with the educational system, but it is due to her doubts about her intelligence. Sagittarius is opposite of Gemini. Where as Gemini gathers information, the Teacher is the philosopher, working to gain a broader understanding of information.

Wounded teacher types can develop unhealthy boundaries with their students (think of Zeus with all of his indiscretions with women). There are a fair amount of spiritual groups where there is inappropriate romantic and sexual interaction between the leaders and followers. Teachers and spiritual leaders must do their own inner work so that they may have healthy boundaries with their students.

Teacher/Travelers love freedom, almost as much as the Idealist. They need freedom of beliefs, freedom in relationships. They often don't look like they will commit to a relationship, but if they are given freedom they will come back to you.

Teachers are good athletes when young, but may become couch potatoes as they age. This is the sign of the archer or centaur, so they often like horses. They can also be very social and "party" in a big way. Jupiter is the largest planet, so anything to do with this archetype is big.

Therapeutic Issues: We sometimes see children with this archetype in therapy with issues around the educational system. Sometimes it is a matter of finding an educational system that holds their interest or has an experiential learning basis.

Dream Images: horses, trains, big trucks or automobiles, schools, anything big.

ELDER LEADER
"ELIZABETH"

Elder Leader (Elizabeth)

Ruled by Saturn in Capricorn. It is a cardinal, feminine Earth sign. It begins winter.

Area of body affiliated with this archetype: The skeleton (structure in the body), the ears, and the knees

History of archetype: The Elder Leader is a feminine energy, but often appears masculine in our patriarchal culture. For example, the archetype is ruled by Saturn and has been traditionally considered a father energy. We call him the Father of Structure. Elder Leader is mature leadership. She is the matriarch.

Mission Statement: To provide Mature Leadership and authority.

Characteristics: This archetype provides cultural leadership as in a tribe or ethnic group. The Elder Leader provides structure, a firm foundation. Saturn constricts. Wherever Saturn is in the astrological chart, there will be a restriction, limitation or an absence. It rules time (Chronos is the Greek correspondent to Saturn). This archetype can sometimes be old when they are young, and young when they are old. It is a death aspect, but more short term than Scorpio, which also has a transformational quality to it. There is a heavy, fearful depressive quality to Saturn.

There is a strong work ethic. This archetype will often stay in the same occupation for many years. Nurses and medical doctors often carry this archetype. The military exemplifies this type of top-down, chain of command leadership. Credentials are important as well as receiving respect, recognition. Traditions are important. If this archetype is involved in a spiritual pursuit, it is usually in an organized religion. As children they want respect and are very vocal if they don't get it.

We are very wounded in our relationship to power and authority. Notice the lack of respect for authority. Many times those in authority abuse their power. This energy can be rigid and controlling, wanting things done her way. "Don't question authority" would be the motto of this archetype in its wounded aspect. And yet, Elder Leader has the potential to lead people with a mature leadership capability, to see a project through to the end. This is the workhorse of the 12 archetypes; it is very responsible in carrying out duties.

Therapeutic Issues: In therapy, we may see domestic violence perpetrators. We would help them give up some of the control they try to maintain over others, particularly intimate partners. The Elder Leader could be a bit more flexible, accepting of situations and people as they are. We would also help him/her recognize that power and authority lie within; the only one they can really control is oneself.

Dream Images: sheep, goats, mountains, tall buildings ice, crystals

THE IDEALIST ~ "EINSTEIN"

Einstein Idealist (Uranus)

Ruled by Uranus in Aquarius. It is a fixed air, male sign. This represents the middle of winter.

Area of body affiliated with this archetype: ankles, calves, circulatory and nervous system. It also shares the respiratory system with Gemini and Virgo.

History of archetype: The visionary who can imagine a better world for all of humanity. Uranus is the Father of Freedom.

We stepped into the Uranian age in 1981 with the conjunction of Jupiter and Saturn, also known as a Syzygy. Carl Jung brought forth this Uranian mystery in his writings. It is the myth of our time, a new understanding.

Mission Statement: The mission of the Idealist is to bring in the New Age, help humanity achieve a higher level of consciousness. It is also the union of opposites: male/female, which characterizes relationships in our time. It is also about Soul integration as there are the two aspects within the Soul: feminine and masculine. The idea is to balance these two energies within oneself.

Characteristics: Idealists are accepting of all humanity, regardless of race, creed, or sexual orientation. They are rather eccentric and exotic looking; Life is a carnival, might as well dress the part. They sometimes play the clown. They are chameleon-like, getting along with all types of people, and yet sometimes they feel alone. They are future oriented. Think of aliens. Idealists get flashes of insight, but then has to go back to explain the steps in getting to that insight. Other people often have a hard time understanding how they got to that conclusion. They will often break structures to gain freedom and will look like a rebel. Teenagers exemplify this energy.

This is a deep soul energy, but can look cool and distant. Idealists are empathetic, but don't cry very easily. They are able to process information in the moment and so move on, while another archetype may still be obsessed by a hurt from the past. They would be good therapists and also good with computers and electronics. This is also the archetype of the pilot, the space traveler.

Sometimes the Idealist can see the ideal so clearly, that they have difficulty dealing with reality. They often need another archetype in the psyche to help them manifest these ideals, such as Elder Leader or Soul Mother, which are practical Earth signs.

Therapeutic Issues: These are the children who are diagnosed with hyperactive, attention deficient disorder. They have a high energy level and a very quick, intuitive mind. They often get bored if not intellectually stimulated. Intense physical exercise helps them direct their abundant energy. It would also be beneficial to involve them in a project and experiential learning, so that they can move around, be involved in their education.

Dream Images: airplanes, dreams of flying.

MYSTIC "MISTY"

Misty Mystic

Ruled by Neptune in Pisces. It is a mutable, feminine, water sign, transitioning from winter to spring.

Area of body affiliated with this archetype: feet, pituitary gland, and immune system.

History of archetype: Jesus, monastic life, monks, and nuns. Yemaya of the African tradition would exemplify the Mystic.

Mission Statement: The mission of the Mystic is to save the world from its pain. There is an urge to merge with other people. Where the Idealist has trouble crying, the Mystic seems to have a need to cry to release emotions. The Idealist is focused on the future, the Mystic on the past.

Characteristics: Mystics are very intuitive, able to feel other people's emotions. So much so, that they often have difficulty setting boundaries with other people: separating their issues from other people's issues. There is an urge to merge with other people, the cosmos, and God/Goddess. But this fantasy is hard to obtain and again it is hard to separate out one's own issues and to distinguish illusion from reality. This, in turn, brings up trust issues because the boundaries are so ill defined. The task for Mystics is to go within themselves, learn to trust themselves rather than get lost in other people or drugs and alcohol.

Mystics also tend to get lost in drugs and alcohol in search of that unitive experience. Or they lose themselves in a relationship, rather than deal with their own issues. They like altered states of consciousness. Connecting to ones own spirituality, or a higher power is key to healing. That's why the Spiritual aspect of AA or any Spiritual connection is so important. Meditation and prayer are more healthy highs than drugs and alcohol.

Mystics are connected to the dream world, the collective unconscious, and the past. Mystics (along with the Artist/Priestess) sometimes hear voices in their head, which emanate from the collective unconscious. The collective unconscious is the part of the psyche common to all of humanity, from which myths, archetypes, and universal images emanate, as well as all the wounds and shadow elements of humanity. It is a repository of all human experience. Often the Mystic has a difficult time distinguishing what material is personal and what comes from the Collective Unconscious.

Mystics are good in business and administration as they can use their intuitive sense to earn a profit. They are also good actors and actresses as they are able to take on the role of another person. This archetype is the most adept at projecting emotions on others and often others project emotions on them.

Therapeutic Issues: If there are addiction issues, these need to be addressed and to connect with a higher power or some kind of spirituality. (See Section III by Elizabeth Cox for a comprehensive discussion of treating addiction issues in therapy.) Mystics (along with the Artist/Priestess) sometimes hear voices in their head, which emanate from the collective unconscious. In therapy we would help them develop ego strength to understand what is personal content and to help transform and heal these voices from the Collective Unconscious. We would also help them with setting boundaries with others and learning to trust themselves.

Dream Images: water, fish, dolphins, and images relating to sleep (unconscious) or bed. Pisces also rules prisons, hospitals, or any similar public institutions.

Elizabeth's Estate

Setting: An old English mansion set on a large estate.

Elizabeth is a matronly woman of seventy years, born at Christmas time in the year of 1931. She inherited the large 12 -bedroom mansion from her mother after she passed away in 1981. Her mother bequeathed the estate to her as she was the oldest daughter and her mother had confidence that Elizabeth would manage the estate well. She has always lived in the house. As a child she roamed the spacious grounds with her siblings and playmates. She married her husband, Arthur in '56 at the age of 25. He was a dashing young actor in theatre. That's what attracted her to him. She soon grew to dislike that debonair air about him. For what attracted her to him, also attracted many other women. Elizabeth had long ago removed him from her suite to his own kingly suites in the South wing. She acknowledged that he was a good father to their two daughters and son, so she opted to keep him in the house. They had a comfortable arrangement.

Elizabeth, being the matriarch that she is, wanted to share her mansion with her family and friends. Besides the estate was very large and needed many people to manage the up keep of the grounds and large mansion. Elizabeth herself wasn't getting any younger. She had osteoporosis and her heart wasn't as strong as it used to be.

Originally there was a person in each of the twelve bedrooms. Well, as you can imagine, there was quite a bit of conflict in the house. Lance positively annoyed everyone, especially his Aunt Sophia, with his deer trophies, gun collection, rolling toolbox and a full set of exercise equipment in the den, especially when all household members wanted to share that room. Romeo and Mercurious (Merc for short) wanted to do more formal entertaining. Somehow the toolbox didn't lend to the ambience.

Lance is Elizabeth and Arthur's son, born April 1. Lance was briefly married to his wife, Xenia. They produced a son, Lance Jr. Lance still has a lot of anger towards Xenia, but he uses a punching bag to dissipate his anger. It saved repairing the wall so often. It was decided in the family meeting to have Lance move his equipment and accoutrements to the renovated chauffeur's quarters in the old carriage house. Lance gladly agreed to this. He needed a little more headspace. It was costly repairing the holes in the wall of his room after he moved out.

The oldest daughter of Elizabeth and Arthur is Inanna (born at the end of April). She is quite the artist in every sense with her painting, dancing and singing. She inherited this from her father, for God knows, Elizabeth doesn't have an artistic bone in her body. Inanna could produce the most exquisite pieces of art, but it left half of the house very messy with fifty different paint jars all over the kitchen and formal dining room. Inanna discovered an old artist studio on the property. With a little renovating and cleaning up she now has a beautiful studio with a loft and a view of the countryside to inspire her artwork. She also has a small kitchen where she keeps a stash of her favorite sweets and desserts. She could indulge her sweet tooth without Sofia's lecture on health or Lance's offer to take her jogging. Right, maybe if someone were chasing her, she would run. She also discovers that she is a little more creative in her own quiet space.

Aunt Sophia (Elizabeth's younger sister) had enough of people, period. She longed for a quiet place where she could think, where her cat could roam at will. She renovated the Caretaker's Cottage into her own private sanctuary. She cleaned out the massive fireplace and built a warm hearth. She planted a year around garden in the green house, including her healing herbs. She developed a well-stocked pharmacy. Her sister Sabrina uses the herbs in attending to the other members of the estate when they are ill. She now has her own small library full of her favorite books. She now receives some of her private clients, for whom she provides holistic counseling, incorporating physical, emotional, mental, and spiritual aspects in her work. She has her own small kitchen where she can prepare healthy, holistic food.

Elizabeth has an older brother nicknamed Einstein because of his creative genius. He is constantly experimenting with his newest theory in his lab. He has some great ideas on how to improve humanity's existence on the planet. The only problem is that the lab was adjacent to his sleeping room and he was constantly blowing up his experiments. This also became costly in repairing the room. Einstein gladly agreed to move to the hangar on the property, where he has his two aircraft. He was a WWII pilot. He likes vintage planes. One of the rooms in the hangar easily converted to a sleeping room and another to a laboratory. He found he had much more freedom in his own abode.

The Professor, or Prof as he is fondly called, decided he would have better access to his mare, Sophia, if he moved to the groom's quarters. She was due to foal in a couple of months and he wanted to be available for the momentous occasion. He converted one room to his private library where he kept his great collection of books and artifacts collected from around the world. He still is an avid traveler, traveling internationally at least once a year. He retired from the local university where he taught Anthropology and Philosophy for 20 years. He still has contact with many of his students, some of whom have become renowned in their line of work. The Prof has also published many of his own books as well as works by other authors.

Well, that left a bit more room in the mansion for the others to live a little more comfortably. Elizabeth had her rooms, including a study in the north wing. Her sister, Sabrina, occupied the rooms in the west wing, where she could be close to her older sister. Sabrina is a midwife and a hospice worker, attending people dying of AIDS. As Elizabeth ages, Sabrina also attends to her dear older sister, using some of Sophia's herbs.

Elizabeth's second daughter Misty, born in the cold month of February, drinks like a fish. She had converted the room next to her sleeping quarters into a bar, of all things. She inherited this trait of imbibing too much from her father, although her father had a bit more control over his consumption than his unfortunate daughter. Misty also has difficulty setting boundaries with others. She seems to feel the pain of the world, which led to crying spells and of course, more drinking. Try as she might, Elizabeth couldn't get her daughter to quit drinking. She had come to a point of resignation over this, relinquishing control to her daughter. Misty also resides in the East Wing where her mother and aunt could keep an eye on her, lest she fall and not be able to get up.

Arthur (Elizabeth's estranged husband) resides in the south wing. He was a director of the theatre, having been an actor for many years previously. He was well liked and had many friends. He was constantly conversing on the phone or going to the theatre. In more recent years, he produced a play every summer in the open-air theatre on the estate. This year he was directing a play he wrote entitled "The Twelve Archetypes", based on work by Carl Jung and his friend Charles Bebeau.

Romeo and Mercurious reside in the east wing. The two of them developed a public relations business and converted two rooms on the ground floor to their offices. They discovered they could work in tandem, Merc servicing the accounts of clients and Romeo managing the public relations. At one time Romeo had courted Misty, but she drank way too much for him to consider a more intimate or long-term relationship. She let him know her alcohol had precedence over him.

These two men, along with Arthur in the south wing, are the more social members of the estate. Once the dreadful guns, exercise equipment, saddles, exploding laboratory were out of the manor, they could entertain lavishly and as often as they liked. Romeo had a knack for bringing the great ballroom and formal gardens to life again after almost a decade of idleness and neglect. Romeo found a great ally in Mama in providing refreshments for the guests.

Mama has been the cook for Elizabeth's family for as long as Elizabeth can remember. Mama loved feeding people, the more the merrier. The twelve inhabitants of the estate still dine together often in the formal dining room. Mama, who has her quarters off of the great kitchen and pantry, still presides over the cooking, although she readily accepts help from the others. Mama is a great bosomy woman, who seemed to sense others' presence and emotions through some mysterious body sense. Many people find comfort in her arms and from her nourishing food.

All was going well on the estate until Elizabeth took a turn for the worse. She called everyone to her room to say her good byes. Misty was devastated. Sobbing, she promised her mother that she would quit drinking. She promised to convert the bar to an altar, get involved with AA, find her higher power, and find sober friends.

That night Elizabeth died. Sabrina and Sophia emphasized to the others the importance of saying goodbye and completing the grief process, allowing oneself to be sad, feel all the emotions, and not repress them. Misty quickly readied the Chapel on the grounds. Elizabeth's body was laid out in her favorite dress. Misty said, "Doesn't she look wonderful? She loved that dress."

Merc, always the logical one, took it upon himself to correct that misperception. "No, Misty, she doesn't look good. She's dead." He personally thought that when you were dead, you were dead. What was all the fuss about? Better live life while he could. When he was gone, he was gone. No more cruising around town, talking to friends. He'd better do his socializing now.

The friends all decided that Elizabeth would want them to have a good time. There was a lot of food and music. Misty also spruced up the old ferry house and they went canoeing on the small pond on the estate. They played volleyball on the green and danced to the band.

And who became the new owner of the estate? Elizabeth bequeathed the estate to the remaining eleven. They, of course, would need to find a twelfth person, a woman, an elder leader, so that all twelve of the archetypes will be represented on the estate and in the psyche.

Summary of Part I and II

By now my readers are probably asking themselves how this applies to them and their lives. How does this all tie together? I would suggest that the most important thing is to begin to be familiar with your own inner life: your dreams, thoughts, and feelings. Begin by keeping a journal about your thoughts, feelings, and situations that occurred during your day. A journal is your best friend. You can tell it things you wouldn't tell anyone else and it doesn't judge you. You may find that it helps you dissipate some of your anger, rather than saying something you later regret. It can also help you sort out your thoughts.

In that journal begin recording your dreams. Even if you don't usually remember your dreams, giving yourself the suggestion to do so, may help you to begin to remember them. As you record the dream, notice any of the archetypal themes I have listed under the description of each archetype. Circle a word that describes the archetype.

Next, notice if the dream image is the same gender as oneself or if the opposite gender is present. Is there conflict in the dream or is it harmonious, even some sex involved? If it involves you or the same gender and there is conflict, it is level one. If it is harmonious, even involves some sex, or innuendo, it is level two. If it involves the opposite gender and it is conflictual, it is level three. If it is harmonious and involves sex and possibly the birth of a baby, it is level four. Record the archetype and the level following the dream you have written. Also notice what kinds of feelings you have upon waking, any situations in your life, or any body symptoms. You will begin to be more in touch with your inner life.

The archetypes have taught me to accept and appreciate everyone as an individual. (At least I attempt to do that, as I haven't obtained perfection yet). I attempted to demonstrate in the play the manner in which each archetype would react to a given situation, in this instance, living in the same residence. If we can allow each archetype to express their personality in a style that is comfortable to them, we will have more harmony and acceptance among us. Although families will carry some of the same archetypes, we all know how different one sibling can be from another one. It is important to allow each child to pursue his/her interests in life. Each child will also have a peculiar learning style that we must honor. Children will not always follow in their parent's foot -steps as far as occupational interests. We can apply this concept to the world as a whole, recognizing the differences in religions, customs, dress, etc. Perhaps there would be more peace and less war.

Finally, it is important to honor the ebb and flow of one's emotional life. There will be ups and downs and difficulties in one's life. We can learn to be more comfortable and accepting of these cycles. To know oneself and to accept and love oneself is the greatest accomplishment of all. When we think someone else is treating us badly, it is worth investigating whether we are treating ourselves badly. At times it is also helpful to find a good therapist to help guide one through life.

Part III

One Practical Application Of Jungian Archetypal Psychotherapy: Addiction Relapse Prevention With the Mystic Archetype

By Elizabeth Cox, M.A.

So what hope is there for the "Mistys" of the world, but a slow and socially disgraceful death? We've all known or loved one such friend, co-worker or family member. We've tried in vain to cajole, bribe or threaten them with the ultimatums to separate them from their substance of choice for getting high: alcohol, drugs, cigarettes, food, gambling, shopping or sex, "for their own good,"

Or perhaps we sent them to a 12-step program.

Since the inception of Alcoholics Anonymous, the first 12 Step program, in 1935 by a New York stockbroker and an Akron physician, many 12 Step groups have grown exponentially to include Narcotics Anonymous, Overeaters Anonymous and others too numerous to mention. All are based on the original 12 Steps of recovery from the "seemingly hopeless state of mind and body" (Big Book, p. xiii) known as alcoholism, put in today's therapeutic terms, the Disease Model. The 12 Steps are outlined below:

1. We admitted we were powerless over alcohol—that our lives had become unmanageable.
2. Came to believe that a Power greater than ourselves could restore us to sanity.
3. Made a decision to turn our will and our lives over to the care of God as we understood Him (or Her).
4. Made a searching and fearless moral inventory of ourselves.
5. Admitted to God, to ourselves, and to another human being the exact nature of our wrongs.
6. Were entirely ready to have God remove all these defects of character.
7. Humbly asked Him to remove all our shortcomings.
8. Made a list of all persons we had harmed, and became willing to make amends to them all.
9. Made direct amends to such people whenever possible, except when to do so would injure them or others.
10. Continued to take personal inventory, and when we were wrong, promptly admitted it.
11. Sought through prayer and meditation to maintain conscious contact with God as we understood Him, praying only for knowledge of His will and the power to carry that out.
12. Having had a spiritual awakening as a result of these steps, we tried to carry this message to alcoholics, and to practice these principles in all our affairs.

By 1941, AA had grown to 8,000 members and become a national institution. From this increase in size, evolved the 12 traditions that laid out the governing principles of the organization and created unity worldwide. The first edition of the "Big Book," the organization's Bible outlining the recovery program, first appeared in April 1939, written by Dr. William D. Silkworth, AA's medical benefactor.

The origin of the AA movement is inherently spiritual. Six months before the inspired talk between Dr. Bob and Bill W., AA's co-founders, Bill W. "had been relieved of his drinking obsession by a sudden spiritual experience." (Big Book, p. XV) With the help of New York alcohol specialist Dr. William Silkworth, Bill W. became convinced of "the need for moral inventory, confession of personal defects, restitution to those harmed, and necessity of belief in and dependence upon God." (Big Book, p. XVI)

The first meeting of Bill W. and Dr. Bob in June 1935, each with his awareness of the need for a spiritual solution, combined with the medical research on alcoholism done by Dr. William Silkworth as the basis for setting AA in the Disease Model. The meeting also established the tradition that it takes one alcoholic/addict to help another, based on this discovery by both founders, who had each been unable to maintain his sobriety alone.

Since the founding of AA over 65 years ago, its meeting format remains simple and personal. "Each day, somewhere in the world, recovery begins when one alcoholic talks with another alcoholic, sharing experience, strength and hope" (Big Book, p. XXII).

For many, 12 Step programs will not be the ultimate solution to relapse prevention, for they come to resent the equally powerful dependency on the program itself. Some are unwilling to surrender to the belief in the Disease Model that one is sick in mind, body and spirit. For others, their problem is with the God principle.

A Certain percentage will find satisfaction in various other movements such as Rational Recovery, Moderation Management, and various empowerment groups that help people limit their drinking, and the remainder of those who do recover often simply outgrow their dependency and quit on their own. [15]

But the remaining group of alcoholics and addicts are my concern here. They are the "closet Mystics," unknowingly carrying the energy of the Mystic Archetype, with their tendency to deal with life's difficulties by narcotizing themselves or wanting to "get high" when necessary to separate themselves from the pain of their negative emotions. Is there a cure for them, bent on slow, painful self-destruction?

The Mystic archetype, as exemplified by the character Misty in Theresa Bauer's play, would be referred to an archetypal psychotherapist for relapse prevention. This practitioner looks at Misty as a whole person, at her state of wellness or dis-ease at each level—body, mind, spirit and emotions, and begins with an intake quite different from the typical information gathering of historical data that is usually done by most therapists.

The type of information gathered at the Archetypal Psychotherapist's intake would include the following: physical illnesses, surgeries, broken bones, injuries, or diseases, birth date, time place, history of family of origin and siblings, strengths, weaknesses, previous counseling experiences, and substance use, and finally, four wishes. From this preliminary data, the person's natal chart would be constructed, identifying the major archetypal rulerships inherent in the person's individual astrological profile.

Misty personifies the Mystic Archetype distinguished by strong psychic energy, mystical visions and emotional turbulence. Misty at first appears victim-like in presenting symptoms of addiction, co-dependency, and low self-esteem, with tendencies toward emotional obsession, lack of trust and setting boundaries in relationships with others.

The connection to water is clearly shown, for this archetype is associated with that element through the sign of Pisces and the planet Neptune. Thus, Misty presents drowning in her own sorrow and self-pity. She is tormented, feeling that others are running her life, pressuring her to change. She claims to trust no one any longer, for they have all disappointed her. She depends on alcohol because it's the best friend that she has, one who has always been there for her.

She has no faith in herself, and in her longing for union, she has entered into a long series of relationships, wherein each man appeared to be her potential "soul mate." She is drawn to them by her all-consuming "urge to merge," and ultimately feels frustrated when the fantasy figure of her obsessions disappoints her simply by manifesting his human limitations. She deftly voids the union with self that could free her from this cycle.

She reports feeling relief most profoundly at those times when she extends herself to help another, for the archetypal psychotherapist knows that her true mission is to save the world from its pain. In those moments, she is so deeply touched by the empathy she feels for her suffering fellow human being, that she experiences the sensation of "getting high" from the deep union of dissolving into the Other.

The archetypal psychotherapist's approach, on the first visit following the intake, is to address physical, mental, spiritual and emotional needs, beginning with the body. She observes that Misty looks sad, sullen and dejected. On the verge of tears as she sits, wrapped in her sweater with arms folded around

---

[15] Marianne Gilliam, *How Alcoholics Anonymous Failed Me*, (William Morrow & Co., 1998), p. 269.

herself. She says she doesn't know if she wants to go on, she feels like a failure: she's tried to stop drinking but can't stay stopped.

Misty's current coping skills include self-medication as the only route to soothing herself. The archetypal psychotherapist first assesses for lethality by determining the degree of severity of her suicidal ideations. Misty admits to having no plan, but feeling life isn't worth living, and that she wishes she could drink herself to death eventually. When pressed, she admits she would choose pills, if she had enough to do the job right.

The archetypal psychotherapist understands that the Mystic energy, which Misty carries, is often murky, foggy and confused. Responding to the seriousness and urgency of the symptoms, the therapist invites Misty to consider that is not necessarily the physical body she wants to die, but some of the dreams or illusions she has been living and accepting as reality. She reads to her from a book based on ancient Toltec wisdom.

> "The mind is divided as the body is divided…the mind can talk to itself. Part of the mind is speaking and the other part is listening…each one has different thoughts and feelings: each one has a different point of view. Your whole mind is a fog…a dream, and illusion. It is the personality's notion of 'I am.' Everything you believe about yourself and the world, all the concepts and programming you have in your mind…we cannot see who we truly are…we cannot see that we are not free. That is why humans resist life. To be alive is the biggest fear humans have. Death is not the biggest fear humans have: our biggest fear is taking the risk to be alive—the risk to be alive and to express what we really are. Just being ourselves is the biggest fear of humans. We have learned to live our life satisfying other people's demands. We have learned to live by other people's points of view because of the fear of not being accepted and of not being good enough for someone else.
> 16

With this, Misty's eyes reflect some inner knowing, she appears to respond on an intuitive level to the passage. The therapist then asks Misty what is making her so afraid to be alive—what beliefs about herself, or agreements that she has made with others based on those beliefs are causing her suffering. She asks Misty to consider that perhaps it is these outgrown or dead aspects of Self that no longer serve her that she is wishing would die.

The archetypal psychotherapist then asks Misty if that would be an acceptable compromise for how she is feeling at this time. That is, if she could find a way to help Misty die to those worn out beliefs about Self and agreements she made that no longer fit the Self she wants to be, and a way to allow for the birth of the new Self, would she be willing to enter willingly into that process of death and rebirth, descent and ascent we call growth.

Misty leaves the second session feeling safe, but unsure of how she will respond to the therapist's invitation to engage fully in the work laid out before her of becoming whole and forsaking the role of victim. The secondary gains have been great; for she has been able to blame others when she has done things their way and things have not worked out to her liking. She is now being asked to take complete responsibility for her life and her process.

In the meantime, the therapist draws up the treatment plan for Misty. First, she addresses the depression, which Misty is self-medicating with alcohol, itself, a depressant, thus aggravating the original condition. She acknowledges that it would be simple enough to send Misty to her PCP for an anti-depressant, since she meets the criteria: the condition has persisted for at least six months, and the client has a family history of depression.

[16] Don Miguel Ruiz, *The Four Agreements, A Practical Guide to Personal Freedom*; (Amber-Allen Publishing, San Rafael, California), p. 16-17.

"Although experts aren't sure what causes depression, research shows that a family history of the disease can raise your risk. Scientists also suspect that depression is due to a chemical imbalance of these "feel good" hormones: serotonin, dopamine, and noradrenaline. And excessive stress can sometimes trigger changes in your brain's chemistry." [17]

Misty also does not have the classic symptoms of depression outlined in the DSM-IV, the mental-health bible of disorders: persistent loss of interest and pleasure in activities that were once enjoyable; sleep or appetite changes; difficulty concentrating or making decisions, though she does feel low self-esteem and a sense of worthlessness and guilt and flagging energy.

Misty is also at higher risk due to her gender. Recent statistics show that the mental illness affects twice as many women as men, according to Shari Lusskin, M.D., of New York University Medical Center[18]. In 1999, more than 4 million women between ages 20 and 35 were given prescriptions for antidepressants... Since September 11, prescriptions written for SSRIs (Selective Serotonin Reuptake Inhibitors) like Zoloft, Paxil and Prozac jumped 3.5 percent, according to NDC Health, a health-information service company in Atlanta. [19]

Since Misty is hesitant about trying medication, due to her tendency to abuse any more substances, but she is enthusiastic about using a natural approach to health, consciousness and healing, the therapist outlines the following plan to be successful "going natural" to elevate mood. Misty is to focus on two major areas—exercise and nutrition. The therapist pointed out that Misty, in search of a quick fix, should soon see results.

"One study showed that 30 minutes of daily activity lifted spirits in just 10 days; another found that people who eat fish at least twice a week were less apt to get depressed than those who eat it less often. An amino acid called 5-hydroxy L-tryptophan supplement helps boost serotonin production (found in turkey and milk) and may also help fend off a funk." The therapist offered these recent findings.[20]

The therapist also gave her some other research tips about breaking out of a bad mood: eat fatty fish (tuna, salmon, mackerel) containing omega-3 fatty acids found in huge concentrations in the part of your brain that affects serotonin activity; cut down on sugar and caffeine that provide a quick high followed by a crash; give up cigarettes for good, (research shows that nicotine causes your brain to produce extra dopamine, giving the temporary rush, but women who smoke are more likely to have a depressive illness).

Cardio-vascular exercise three times a week gets blood flowing to the brain and has been shown to be as effective as psychotherapy in treating depression. Folic Acid, a B vitamin in a 400 mcg. Supplement, can treat mild depression; an herbal remedy, St. John's Wort in the recommended dose of 900 mg. Per day (side effects of hypertension and increased sensitivity to sunlight) and the supplement SAM-e, naturally occurring in our cells, that helps regulate serotonin and dopamine with possible side effects of nausea and insomnia and mania [21]were all presented to Misty as natural alternatives to antidepressant prescription medication.

Misty loved the idea of being on the cutting edge of a new movement, those seeking the "natural highs" instead of the old guard looking for the quick fix of a pill. Recently the Journal of the American Medical Association (J.A.M.A.) reported that between 1987 and 1997, the number of Americans being treated for depression more than tripled, from 1.8 million to 6.3 million, while those taking antidepressants doubled. The vast majority of those antidepressants are SSRIs.[22]

In contrast, the J.A.M.A study reports that over the same 10-year period, the percentage of patients in therapy dropped from 71.1% to 60.2% and the average number of annual treatment visits declined from 12.6 to fewer than nine. The danger inherent in such statistics is that we throw pills at problems rather than grapple with the underlying causes.[23]

---

[17] Marie Claire *"Is it more than the Blues?"* (Self, Dec.2001); p. 152.

[18] Ibid.

[19] *"Are We Happy Yet, Rethinking the Prozac Revolution:"*(Self, Dec. 2001), p.100.

[20] Ibid.

Aware of this trend, Misty's therapist points out that she wants their visits to continue throughout the six months Misty is withdrawing from alcohol and beginning this behavior change program, if not the entire first year. She would like to see Misty weekly for the first 90 days, and a minimum of every two weeks for the second three-months. Misty reports feeling encouraged by this support for her during this challenging time.

The therapist points out that the results Misty will get from improving her diet and incorporating exercise will be surprising and dramatic. She shows Misty a recent article from the newspaper[24] citing a study by Duke University psychologist James Blumenthal in Durham, N.C. of 156 volunteers with clinical depression to test the effectiveness of exercise and other treatment strategies. Patients were divided into three groups:

1. Antidepressants only.
2. Antidepressants plus aerobics (30 minutes, three times a week).
3. Exercise only.

After 16 weeks, patients in all three groups were equally likely to have recovered: about two-thirds no longer were depressed. Those on pills were more likely to get better within a month. The patients were free to treat their depression as they saw fit after the 16-week study. The follow-up six months later told the tale.

"The exercisers held the edge. Only 8 percent relapsed to depression, compared with 38 percent who took pills only and 31 percent in the combination group. Overall, 30 percent in the exercise group were still clinically depressed, compared with 52 percent on medication and 55 percent taking antidepressants and exercising. Exercisers who took no pills may feel they alone were responsible for their recovery, and this sense of mastery could improve their long-term prospects for mental health, Blumenthal speculates".[25]

The therapist and Misty then custom-tailored a program of exercise for Misty consisting of yoga, weight training, dance and a water aerobic workout at least
three times a week. The Archetypal Psychotherapist knew that for the Mystic, the key to success is to acknowledge that they are often "spiritual jocks" rather than the gym types. Mystics tend to thrive in or near nature, especially in their element water, and with some kind of "quiet energy" workout that helps ground them, such as Yoga or meditation.

The therapist used yoga because it links two key elements to healing for Mystics—body and breath. Misty was amazed to know that "15 million Americans (twice as many as five years ago) have realized what an incredible workout it can be. Deep energizing breaths combined with fluid movement and challenging poses train your heart and lungs, at the same time you increase flexibility and balance.[26]

Finally, there remained one final yet inherently powerful element of Misty's healing program that was introduced by the Archetypal Psychotherapist—breath work. Misty had no idea what she was in for when she came in for her first breath work session. The therapist had prepared her by telling her to allow 11/2 hours for the treatment. A futon had been opened up and prepared for Misty to stretch out on, and the therapist began.

When the therapist sat down on the floor beside Misty, who was prone on the futon, she asked Misty to close her eyes and do some deep, abdominal breathing without stopping, to work up a good rhythmic intake of breath that would resemble what one would do if running or swimming. The goal is to

---

[21] Claire, *Is It More Than the Blues?*

[22] *"Been down so long..."* (Time, Jan. 21, 2002)

[23] Ibid.

[24] *"Aerobic Exercise May Keep You Saner,"* (The Denver Post, January 16, 2001).

[25] Ibid.

put the client into an altered state—a natural high, and to "drop into the dream state", so as to access the subconscious.

The psychiatrist Carl Jung used the term "numinous" to describe that that does not emanate from the conscious personality; "he calls them from a daimon, a god, or the unconscious".[27] When a person enters the dream-like realm produced by breath work, it is like those who meditate and achieve Nirvana, as the Buddhists refer to the attainment of bliss when the self is lost deep in the meditative state.

Misty came out of her first session of breath work stating "that is the most perfect experience I have had—ever." She was teary, had energy surging through her hands as a tingling sensation, and described the state as incomparable, perhaps as lucid dreaming. She was eager to come in for another treatment, and wondered when she could learn to replicate the experience on her won. The therapist assured her that would come, with practice.

Misty was to have six to eight breath work sessions written into her treatment plan, and at least six were full hour and a half sessions, with the final two being coaching sessions for Misty to practice doing them at home by herself, to see if she could attain the Zen-like, meditative state on her own. By the eighth session, Misty was entirely confident that she would be able to practice breath work on her own at home without a coach.

What Misty realized in processing the results of breath work was that gradually, in combination with the other exercises she was doing, she was altering her metabolism and thus altering her brain chemistry, without drugs. She found that improved nutrition, regular movement such as dance, yoga and aerobic exercise, and finally breath work were producing naturally what Misty had been trying unsuccessfully to do with alcohol.

Since alcohol is a depressant, Misty was only creating a 20-minute high at best before the disappointing and inevitable crash of alcohol. Now she found, after the first 90 days, that she felt her mood consistently elevated from the natural increase in her endorphins raised by proper nutrition and exercise. And unlike alcohol, there was no crash that followed these "uppers".

Breath work had taught her how to put herself into a trance when she needed to induce "feeling high". She found that self-mastery liberating and empowering. She was also delighting in the various forms of dance that Mystics love so well. One night a week, she danced with other women in an improvisational dance group. Another night, she participated in a mixed group in the Dances of International Peace— a movement that also led to an increase in her social life with like-minded individuals also spiritually inclined. The group dances are done to different spiritual traditions around the world in order to emphasis the commonality among all people in the world.

Finally, the aqua aerobics and Yoga had toned her whole body, so that she was feeling fitter and healthier than she ever had in her entire life, by her own jubilant report.

The final phase of Misty's therapy involved improving her relationships with men, and learning to set boundaries and how to create trust so that she ceased to feel like the resentful victim in her interactions, not only with men, but also with everyone else. This was one of the most difficult phases of Misty's recovery, for she had been co-dependent. She claimed to hate the "C-word", but admitted it applied to her in many of her relationships.

Her therapist worked hard with her on her trust issues, as Mystics have particular difficulty with avoiding the trap of merging into the other to achieve the much-desired union, losing themselves, feeling invisible, then resenting the Other for controlling them. The Other can't win, and neither can the relationship be successful without boundaries, for where does the Other end and Misty begin?

The therapist recommended two books for Misty to read on the subject, *Boundaries: Where You End and I Begin*, by Anne Katherine[28] and *"No" Is a Complete Sentence: Learning the Sacredness of*

---

[26] *"Power Up Your Yoga"*, (*Shape*, p.136-137; March, 2002).

[27] C.G. Jung edited by Aniela Jaffe, *Memories, Dreams and Reflections*, (Vintage Books, Random House, New York), P. 336.

Personal Boundaries. [29] Misty and the therapist discussed the inherent difficulties for Misty in shifting from setting no limits to defining boundaries in relationships so that she began to feel a new sense of freedom and self-respect.

With Misty's strong desire for union in relationships with men she liked, it was difficult for her initially to see the therapist's wisdom in referring her to a sensible approach recommended by a famous female TV talk show host who found a workable solution to the expectation of casual sex that is now a part of today's dating scene. Iyanla Banzant, author of 11 books (3 are national best sellers), lawyer and formerly single parent share her thoughts on romances that stand a chance: "I have a 90-day rule. When you're going into a relationship with another person, you should delay physical intimacy—we're talking sex here—for 90 days. And use that 90-day period to get to know who he is. Talk about things. Share your thoughts and feelings.[30] Since Misty has set this boundary, she now has confidence and security.

Discharge Notes and Follow Up: At a recent interview with Misty, she reports that she has been sober for a year, and has had no relapses, and no cravings. She is exploring new ways to maintain her sobriety, from AA meetings, to Rational Recovery. She has not yet decided on one type of group, but continues to try more than one means of joining together with other recovering alcoholics for strength and support.

Misty has more than one dating relationship, and is enjoying taking her time getting to know men on a slower track, and not being so hasty about jumping into relationships. She has increased her self-esteem by not engaging in sex prematurely, before laying the groundwork for emotional intimacy. She has also learned how to speak up for herself when anyone violates her personal boundaries.

Finally, Misty radiates a new vibrant glow of health since adopting new life-affirming behaviors. She has lost the pasty look of the poorly nourished alcoholic, and exchanged it for the natural clear-eyed beauty she always was underneath. Everyone complements her on her youthful appearance, and asks what's different about her. She smiles and tells them that she is recovering from an illness that almost took her life. She credits her Archetypal Psychotherapist for treating her as a whole person, not merely as having an addiction problem. For this therapist was willing to address her problems on every level of her being—mental, physical, spiritual and emotional. As a result, the comprehensive treatment planning helped the client through the total recovery process. This is an alternative to the more one-dimensional cognitive-behavioral approach.

Perhaps one reason the cognitive-behavioral approach is not successful in preventing relapse is that it focuses primarily on the physical and mental aspects of the person's being. Alcoholism is a problem that compromises a person on every level of existence; spiritual and emotional as well as mental and physical. Therefore, the whole person must be rehabilitated. Archetypal Psychotherapy takes the wholistic approach, with an emphasis on the spiritual, befitting the Mystic Archetype.

---

[28] (Fireside/Parkside Recovery Book 1999).

[29] (Ballantine Books, New York 1995).

[30] *"Making It Last,"* (*Health,* September 2001), p. 162.

Part IV

Jungian Archetypal Analysis from an Astrological Point of View

By Theresa Bauer LPC, CAC III, with Charles Bebeau PhD.

This section of the book is written from an astrological point of view and is designed to allow you to discover your ruling archetypes (archetypes predominant within you). It is based on Dr. Charles Bebeau's work of Jungian Archetypal Psychology. We are attempting to make this brilliant and unique work as easily understandable and accessible as possible.

Determining Your Ruling Archetypes

Astrology is an ancient art that was practiced by the Hebrews since prehistoric times (See Rabbi Joel C. Dobin, D.D., Kabbalistic Astrology: The Sacred Traditions of the Hebrew Sages, Vt.: Inner Tradition, 1999.) In this analysis we will interpret the chart similar to the manner used by Jewish astrologers. They gave a lot of importance to the rising planets; in other words, the planets rising in the Eastern horizon at the moment of birth. We will also add an archetypal dimension to it. We have attempted to make this interpretation as easy as possible.

This analysis utilizes a traditional astrology chart. You may obtain one at several sites on line or at many metaphysical bookstores. Also Matrix makes a software program called Win star, which allows you to create your own charts. We use a geocentric, tropical Koch house system

I (Theresa) believe this is a tool for self-discovery and awareness. I have found it useful in my private practice as a mental health and substance abuse therapist. I think the main concept I have gotten out of this work, is that we are all unique individuals and that we aren't cookie cutter models of each other. Some of us will like relationships better than others; some like their quiet time; others enjoy cooking, art; some people are athletic, while others abhor any sort of exercise. We aren't all going to like the same thing or invoke the same experiences in our lives. I don't think we so much become well rounded, in that we are "jack of all trades". It is more like we are master of one or several. Although for some people, maybe being a jack-of-all-trades is what they are about.

Archetypes are energy patterns in humanity that have existed since the beginning of human history. This theory states that we all carry within us different archetypes, which helps define our personalities, including, our likes and dislikes. This is merely a blue print. We fill in the pieces; make our own decisions and choices, but some of the patterns we are born with. There are 12 total archetypes in this system. We will all carry a bit of each of the twelve archetypes within us, but will have 4, 5, 6, and sometimes 7 of these archetypes more strongly within us. (Idealists tend to have more archetypes as they are like chameleons and get along with a variety of people.) These are called ruling archetypes.

Each archetype has its strength and it's shadow. Shadow is defined as personality traits that we don't recognize in ourselves, whether they are positive or negative. Sometimes an individual may have the potential to be a leader; they see it in someone else, but don't see that in their self. They project their ability on someone else. This is also a shadow aspect, in that it is hidden, unacknowledged in the individual. We are all projection machines. The mission is to take back the projection, own it ourselves and work with it; to become the potentiality that we see in others.

Each archetype has a wounded aspect to it. When we embody that archetype, we may also carry that wound. This mission is to heal that archetype within us, which in turn heals the collective psyche. For example the Soul Mother and Dark Mother archetypes were present in the women branded as witches and burned at the stake in medieval times. A person carrying either one of these archetypes will likely have a greater sensitivity and awareness of this persecution (wounded aspect) as well as the strength of being aware of human rights and qualities of being a healer. The wounded aspect could result in this person tending to be withdrawn from others to avoid being hurt (Soul Mother) or being secretive and rage full (Dark Mother). The mission of each archetype is to enhance the strengths within oneself and then heal and integrate the wounded aspect within oneself, which in turn heals the collective unconscious.

This theory takes a very optimistic, non-blaming view of humanity. We live in a violent, chaotic world, as well as a beautiful and loving world. Since there has been so much violence and trauma throughout history, it only stands to reason that there are shadow elements or unhealed parts of our society, families and within us. Our mission is to begin to heal this.

Archetypes manifest through our personalities, our dreams, and body symptoms. It is impossible to list all the subtleties of each archetype, but we hope this, at least, is a starting point. Please feel free to use your own intuitive abilities in this adventure into oneself. Also be aware that no one is purely one archetype. Also you will have some of the characteristics of an archetype and not others. You are a unique combination of the different archetypes within you.

There is also a family soul pattern; there are primary archetypes that are carried in a family through generations. We will marry and be involved with people who carry some of the same archetypes as we do. Our children will have some of the same archetypes, even if we adopt them or they are stepchildren or if the birth was induced. Archetypal patterns within us attract other people who have similar archetypal patterns. The Universe uses us (humanity) to carry on the Family Soul as manifested by the 12 archetypal patterns. We are here to manifest that pattern and to heal and transform the shadow aspects of that archetype within ourselves and ultimately in the world.

The Chart

With this short introduction, let us begin. Obtain you're astrological chart from whatever source you decide to. Next place it in front of you. This is a map of the heavens at the moment you were born. Notice that the chart is divided into 12 sections of 30 degrees each. These divisions are called houses. Each one of the zodiacal signs rules a house.

The 1st house begins at the eastern horizon (left side of the chart) and is ruled by Aries, which represents personal power, one's identity (how one sees oneself), and physical appearance. We call the personality the ego/body because there is a mind/body connection. One's thoughts and emotions manifest throughout the body, sometimes through physical ailments or symptoms. The ascendant is also indicative of our physical appearance. Although Aries rules the 1st house, it may not be the sign on the cusp of the 1st house. The sign changes every 2 hours. Aries rules the 1st house symbolically.

The 2nd house is below the 1st house in a counter-clockwise direction and is ruled by Taurus, etc. Any planets in the lower half of the chart (from the 1st house to the 6th house) were below the Earth at the moment you were born.

A person with a majority of planets below the horizon or in the lower half of the chart will tend to be introverted. The planets are distributed in a unique pattern because their orbits around the sun take different amounts of time. Mercury orbits the sun in 88 days and Pluto's orbit is 247 years. Dane Rudhyar's books on astrology (CRCS Publications, Sebastopol, Ca.) are an excellent source of knowledge on astrology.

A person with a majority of the planets above the horizon (from the 7th house to the 12th house) will tend to be extroverted. If the planets are evenly distributed, this person will have qualities of both extroversion and introversion. Introverts replenish their psychic energy within themselves or by being alone. Extroverts energize themselves by being around other people.

There are 4 cardinal points on the chart. The 1st we talked about on the eastern horizon. This is the ascendant. The cusp (line dividing the 3rd and 4th houses) of the 4th house represents mother, home, family background. This corresponds to the midnight position of the chart. (The sun would have to be located here for you to be born at midnight.) The 7th house cusp represents intimate relationships. It is the western horizon. The 10th house cusp represents our work, credentials in the work world. It is in the noon position. (Again the sun would be located there if you were born at noon.)

Following is a simplified chart that shows the houses and cardinal points in a chart. An easy way to remember the cardinal points is that the ascendant represents self; the descendant is other; the nadir is inner life and the midheaven is the outer life.

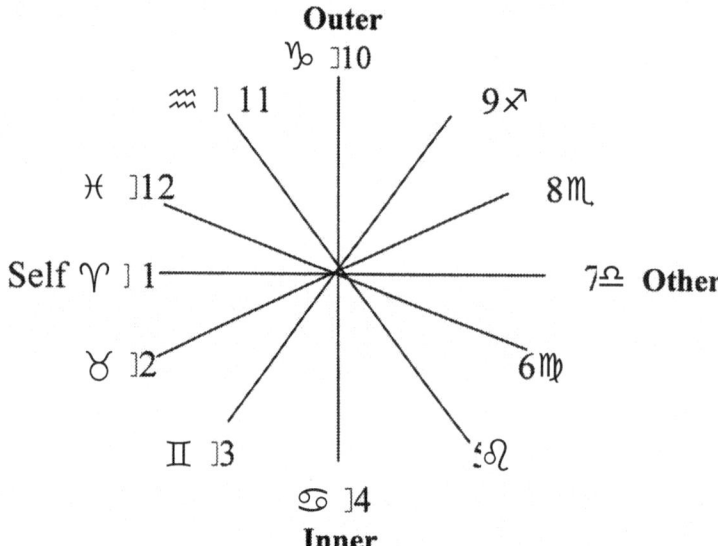

Figure 2

Figure 3 demonstrates the different signs, the planets they are associated with (rulership), the house they are associated with and the gender of the sign. All signs are associated with a gender in traditional astrology, but both men and women can have traits of both feminine and masculine signs and archetypes. One of the basic tenets of Jungian theory is that men have an inner feminine called the anima and women have an inner masculine called the animus.

This concept isn't as odd as you may think at first. After all men often have a very nurturing side to them. In fact, that is often what women fall in love with. When men can be gentle and nurturing with children, women, and other people, it is a strong characteristic. Feminine energy is associated with seeing the whole picture, thinking in terms of relationship, how everyone will benefit from an action.

Women, on the other hand, are demonstrating a strong animus when they develop a career in the work world. Masculine energy is usually associated with linear, logical thinking.

The symbols for the planets consist of ancient symbols intuited by ancient astrologers. Symbols are powerful as they communicate directly with the psyche. The astrological symbols all consist of either the circle O, which represents the masculine principle or the Sun; the crescent ☽, which is the feminine aspect or the moon; or the cross †, which is physical manifestation or the ascendant. We refer to these 3 principles as the trinity of the chart.

Symbols of the Zodiac

Figure 3 illustrates the different symbols of the zodiac and of the planets that rule them.

House	Symbol/Sign	Planet ruled by	Gender	Element	Archetype
1	♈ Aries	♂ Mars	Masculine	Fire	Warrior
2	♉ Taurus	♀ Venus	Feminine	Earth	Artist/Priestess
3	♊ Gemini	☿ Mercury	Masculine	Air	Communicator
4	♋ Cancer	☽ Moon	Feminine	Water	Nourishing Mother
5	♌ Leo	☉ Sun	Masculine	Fire	Golden Child
6	♍ Virgo	☿ Mercury	Feminine	Earth	Soul Mother
7	♎ Libra	♀ Venus	Masculine	Air	Lover
8	♏ Scorpio	♇ Pluto	Feminine	Water	Dark Mother
9	♐ Sagittarius	♃ Jupiter	Masculine	Fire	Teacher/Traveler
10	♑ Capricorn	♄ Saturn	Feminine	Earth	Elder Leader
11	♒ Aquarius	♅ Uranus	Masculine	Air	Idealist
12	♓ Pisces	♆ Neptune	Feminine	Water	Mystic

Now we will demonstrate to you how to determine your ruling archetypes. We will use a sample chart to guide you as you perform the same calculations on your own chart. We have named this fictitious person Baby Jane, born November 21, 2002. Charles Bebeau generally rounds all numbers to the next highest number to make it easier to work with. For example, the Sun is at 29°17' (minutes), but I rounded it up to 30°. Drawing your own chart helps you to become familiar with the symbols and you learn it more thoroughly. It helps to just meditate on a chart and become familiar with the pattern of the stars and they way they were placed at the moment of your birth. They tell a story.

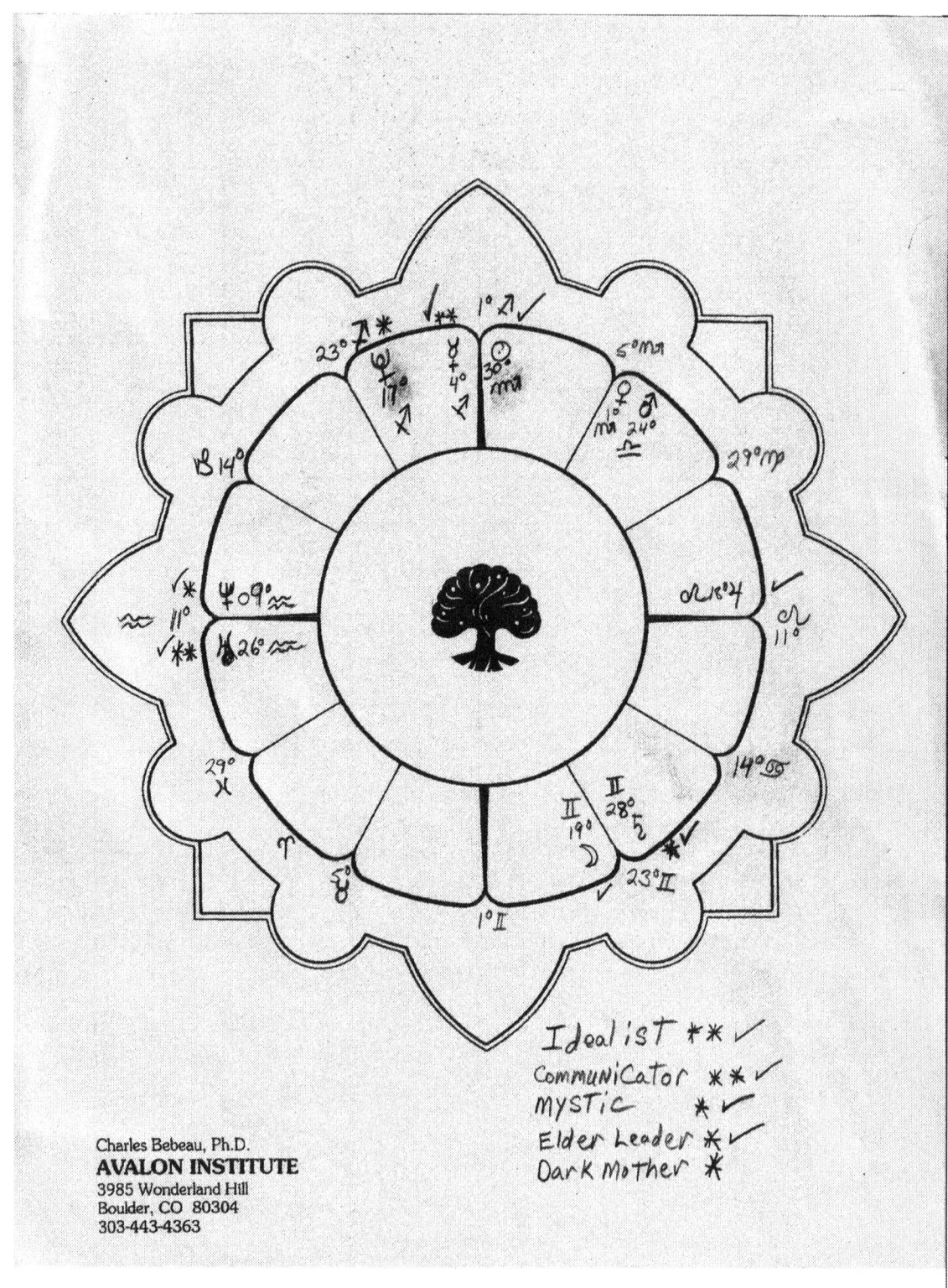

Idealist **✓
Communicator **✓
Mystic *✓
Elder Leader *✓
Dark Mother *

Charles Bebeau, Ph.D.
AVALON INSTITUTE
3985 Wonderland Hill
Boulder, CO 80304
303-443-4363

Level I.

The **first level** of rulership involves any planets that are within 15° (degrees) of the Sun ☉, Moon ☽, and the Ascendant (the trinities).   This called a conjunction ♂.

A. Conjunctions ♂ with the Sun ☉

In our example Mercury ☿ is 4° from the Sun, so it receives an * (asterisk). Remember there are 30° in a sign. The Sun is at 30° Scorpio ♏ or at the last degree in Scorpio. We, then, start into the next sign Sagittarius ♐. Mercury is at 4° Sagittarius, so it is within the 15° limit. There are no other planets that are within 15° of the Sun.

B. Conjunctions ♂ with the Moon ☽

In our example, the moon ☽ is in Gemini ♊. Saturn ♄ is 9°(28-19=9) from the moon, so it also has an Asterisk * placed next to it. There are no more planets near the moon.

C. Conjunctions with the Ascendant

In our example, both Neptune ♆ and Uranus ♅ are within 15° of the ascendant, which is at 11° Aquarius ♒, so those 2 planets have an asterisk placed near them.

Level II. Sign of the Sun ☉, Moon ☽, and Ascendant.

A. Sign of the Sun ☉

In our example the Sun ☉ is in the sign of Scorpio ♏. Pluto ♇ rules Scorpio, so Pluto ♇ has an asterisk * next to it. (The asterisk goes next to the planet, not the sign.)

B. Sign of the Moon ☽

In our example the Moon ☽ is in Gemini. Mercury ☿ rules Gemini so a second * is placed near Mercury ☿.

C. Sign of the Ascendant

In our example, the ascendant is in the sign of Aquarius ♒, so another * is placed near Uranus ♅ , which rules Aquarius.
    A check mark has less of an emphasis than an asterisk, but it is used to add weight in determining rulership. For example, we will look at which planet has the most asterisks and checkmarks in determining rulership.

Level III. Planets in their own sign

In our example, Uranus ♅ is in its own sign of Aquarius ♒, so a check mark √ is placed next to it. For example if Mars ♂ was in Aries ♈, Venus ♀ in Taurus ♉, etc.

Level IV. Planets in their own house

In our example, Neptune is in the 12th house, which is the house that it rules, so Neptune gets a check mark √. (Look at Table I. Notice that Neptune corresponds to the 12th house.)

Sublevels: You can determine rulership by using the above 4 levels. The ones below give it a bit more refinement, but if you find it too confusing, you can still read a chart without going into all the details.

A. Planets on the angles. There is also an emphasis (√) placed on any planets within 7° of the 4th, 7th, and 10th house cusps (these are called the angles of the chart). These planets would receive a check mark (√). In our example, Jupiter ♃ is 7° from the cusp of the 7th house, so it gets a check mark. The Sun ' and Mercury≤ are within 7°of the 10th house cusp (mid heaven), so they also receive a check mark. We have already taken care of the planets by the Ascendant, or the 1st house cusp. In this chart there are no planets conjunct with the Nadir (4th house cusp).

B. What planet rules the house that the Sun ☉   and moon ☽ are in?

The Sun is on the 10th house cusp, so it is considered a 10th house sun. Saturn ♄ rules the 10th house, so it gets a check mark (√). Again the moon is in its own house and has received a check mark for that.

Interpreting Baby Doe's Chart

Now we will pull the ruling archetypes out of Baby Jane's chart. We rank the planets according to which one has the most *'s next to it. The check mark (√) adds weight to the decision. Remember that we look at the planets and from there determine the archetype. Also there are no hard and fast rules in interpreting a chart. Remember to use your intuition as well.

Idealist: Uranus ♅ has **√ next to it, so it is the ruling archetype.

Communicator: Mercury ☿ has ** √ next to it also, but we have put it as number 2 because the Ascendant is stronger. Uranus is by the Ascendant.

Mystic: Neptune ♆ has *√ next to it, so it is the 3rd archetype. It is also by the Ascendant.

Elder Leader: Saturn ♄ has *√ next to it, so it is the 4th archetype.

Dark Mother: Pluto ♇ has * next to it.

Baby Jane will have a rather complex, dynamic personality. She would have a lot of energy with the Idealist archetype. Freedom would be important to her; she would be independent, an intuitive thinker. She might even be labeled with an Attention Deficit Hyperactivity Disorder (ADHD) at a young age. The Communicator archetype would also add to her energy level. Both the Idealist and Communicator are air signs. This represents mental or quick energy. They would tend to think through problems and talk through (Communicator) problems compared to feelers or doers.

Not only would she think and move rapidly, she would also talk rapidly. In her schooling experience, it would be important to give her many stimulating, hands-on experiences. She will be a quick, intuitive learner, but will get restless and bored if not sufficiently stimulated. She will probably be very curious and ask a lot of questions. It will also be important for her to get a lot of exercise to dissipate some of her abundant energy. She may also appear distant or aloof with her Idealist energy. That isn't necessarily true. Idealists process information in the moment and then move on, where some of the Earth signs process information slowly and may hold a grudge. The Idealist has addressed that issue a long time ago and moved on to other things. The Idealist is empathetic, but doesn't find it necessary to go deep into the emotions.

The watery Mystic and Dark Mother will give her a more intense feeling nature. Both of these energies like to go into the depths and explore feelings. The Dark Mother would be concerned with issues around life, death and sexuality. The Mystic would value her connection to other people; possibly even have difficulties setting boundaries, although the Idealist and Elder Leader aspects of herself would help with that task. Both the Idealist and Mystic are on the ascendant, giving her an intuitive edge, the Mystic more feeling-oriented and the Idealist more mental-oriented.

The ascendant represents the ego/body, the personality, and our personal appearance. Baby Jane may have the distant, aloof look of the Idealist or the misty, emotional eyes of the Mystic—or a combination of both. She may also have characteristics of the other archetypes. The Dark Mother also has eyes with a lot of depth that tend to draw a person into them.

The Elder Leader is going to give Baby Jane some structure in her life. She has 3 planets in the 10th house, which also give emphasis to her work, career life. Credentials and advancement in the work place will be important to her. There may be some internal conflicts within her between the Idealist, who is erratic, spontaneous and the Elder Leader, who is practical, structured. Hopefully she will find a good balance between these energies: being creative, intuitive, but using the Elder Leader to ground these energies and being able to follow through with these ideas.

We also notice that Jane has planets distributed all around the chart. She will have traits of both introversion and extroversion, although she may be more extroverted as there are more planets above the horizon (upper part of chart) than below the horizon. The Communicator would be very extroverted and the Mystic would be drawn to people. The Idealist would get along with everyone, something like a chameleon, although they often feel above or beyond other people. Idealists often have many archetypes, like 6 or 7. Jane has an average number with 5 ruling archetypes, although she would have a bit of all 12. We will revisit Jane's chart again as we explore the aspects of the planets.

Aspects of the Planets

In a chart there are lines drawn between planets. These are called aspects of the planets. They denote different relationships to the planets, in addition to the conjunctions we just looked at. Below are some of the symbols and definitions used in astrology to denote the aspects between planets. These definitions draw on traditional astrology plus they have an added meaning as interpreted by Carl Jung and Charles Bebeau.

♂ A **conjunction** occurs when there is 15° (orb) or less between the ascendant, sun, moon and another planet. Conjunctions between two other planets exist when there is 7° or less. A conjunction between 2 planets emphasizes the characteristics of both planets. It is considered a harmonious aspect.

✳ A **sextile** occurs when there are 60° between 2 planets. If you will remember, each sign is identified with a gender, either feminine or masculine. A sextile is two signs apart and will both be either masculine or feminine. For example, a planet in Virgo at 5° and a planet in Scorpio at 5° are sextile. This would be true as well if the planets were in Aries and Gemini. There is an orb of 7°, so a planet, say Mercury could be at 5° Virgo and be sextile to Mars at 12° Scorpio. This is a harmonious aspect within a person, emphasizing the interplay between the 2 planets. .

□ A **square** occurs when there are 90° separating 2 planets, again with an orb of 7°. The 2 planets can produce tension within a person. In other words, there will be tension within this person caused by 2 aspects of his/her personality going 2 different directions. The task of a person with a square is to resolve those differences, so that each aspect can win. The person becomes a stronger, more integrated person for doing this. A square always involves a masculine energy and a feminine energy. There lies the conflict, in that there is much within the gender roles that is wounded and distorted in our society. However, it is possible to integrate these energies into a harmonious whole.

△ A **trine** occurs when there are 120° separating 2 planets, again with an orb of 7°. This produces a social harmony. There is harmony with people outside of oneself involving the energies of these 2 planets. These aspects will involve planets within the same element such as air signs like Aquarius, Gemini, and Libra.

☍ An **opposition** occurs when there are 180° between 2 planets again with an orb of 7°. This produces a social tension. There is tension with other people outside of oneself involving the energies of these 2 planets. Like the square ☐, the mission is to resolve the issue inside of oneself, and then there is a resolution with people outside of oneself. These aspects will involve 2 male signs or 2 female signs like Aquarius-Leo, Scorpio-Taurus.

A **transit** is the relationship between planets on a given day and planets in the natal chart. For example we might look at the relationship of the Sun on March 20, 2003 when it is at 30° Pisces ♓ and baby Jane's Sun at 30° in Scorpio, which forms a trine △ . We mention transits at this point, because the aspects also relate to transits and you can use the information regarding aspects when determining transits.

The following charts demonstrate the aspects between the planets.

The oppositions and squares: The sign opposite it is the opposition ☍ and the signs at a 90° angle are square ☐ .

	♑ Capricorn	
♈ Aries		♎ Libra
	♋ Cancer	

The Cardinal signs are the initiators, the beginning of each season.

	♒ Aquarius	
♉ Taurus		♏ Scorpio
	♌ Leo	

The fixed signs are steadfast, the middle of the season.

	♓ Pisces	
♊ Gemini		♐ Sagittarius
	♍ Virgo	

The mutable signs are flexible, the end of the season, preparing to transition to the next season.

Trines occur between planets in the same elements. This is a harmonious relationship.

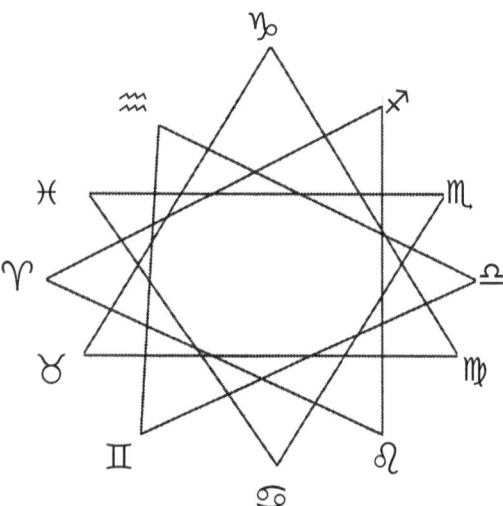

The Cosmic Players

Following is a description of the aspects of the planets (heavenly bodies) to each other, beginning with the Sun and continuing on out to the furthest planet from the Sun, Pluto. Each planet is accompanied by a visual representation or a mythic figure that represents the archetype that that planet rules.

Also there is a descent phase even with harmonious aspects, like the conjunction and trine. The mission with difficult aspects such as the square and opposition is to grapple with the issue and come to terms with it: to get to the acceptance phase.

With that brief description we will begin with the King of the Universe: The Sun, the Golden Child.

Sun ☉ (Golden Child) Aspects

The Sun pertains to the outer worldly Soul Mission; what we do in the world. Soul Mission could be defined as the best example of what a Human can create. Also remember that the Sun in conjunction with any of the planets, gives emphasis to the archetype that the planet rules. Each of the archetypes will have a different mission or purpose in this life, but the Sun pertains to more of the outer mission, what we present to the world. There could be several missions in one's life as each individual has several archetypes. Some of these may be more inner or personal missions. The planets that are conjunct with the Sun as well as the sign of the Sun will determine Soul Mission.

The Sun is a father energy, although symbolically it goes to the Golden Child in this archetypal system. Masculine energy is active and linear in thinking. The Golden Child is dramatic, the king of the universe. The other planets circle around the Sun. The Golden Child represents the interplay between divinity and humanity as the Sun in the heaven touches and energizes us all on the Earth. The Sun also represents our overall health, as the heart rules this archetype.

The Sun also rules the 5th house in the zodiac, which rules love affairs, playful activities, and the children in our lives. It's a fiery, fertile energy; very creative. The Sun would also describe one's relationship to the father's side of the family. For a woman, the Sun tells a story about the men in her life: lovers, father, and sons.

61

Sun/Moon Aspects. ☉/☽

The Moon represents the Nourishing Mother. It is also the feminine body (breasts and stomach). It is a mother energy, representing emotions, the nourishment of others. It is receptive in that it reflects the light of the Sun. Feminine energy uses more of the right hemisphere of the brain. It is more concerned with relationships, how information fits into an overall pattern, mythic and symbolic images, emotions, the body, intuition and it is process -oriented. It is more concerned with the information making up the process than in reaching an immediate solution in a linear, logical manner.

The Sun and the Moon were originally "The Two Lights To Rule by Day and Night."[31] These "two lights" were the starting point of the astrological system. (At one time in the Middle Ages, it was believed that there were only the 7 inner Heavenly bodies. The ancients before Christ's birth knew of the outer planets beyond Saturn, but that information was lost in the Middle Ages. So the Sun and Moon were the starting point with Mercury on either side of them—Gemini, Virgo. Next was Venus in Taurus and Libra. Mars was thought to rule both Aries and Scorpio. Jupiter ruled both Sagittarius and Pisces. Saturn ruled both Capricorn and Aquarius).

Aspects with the Sun and Moon have a 15° orb. Aspects between 2 other planets have a 7° orb.

♂ New moon. When they are in conjunction, they bring out the aspects of the sun and moon. Remember that both the sun and moon bring out the characteristics of any planets within 15° of them. A ♂ of the Sun and Moon bring out the Golden Child/Nourishing Mother aspects in an individual. They are co-rulers; seeding something new. There is a conception between the masculine and the feminine within oneself. This is a creative individual.

☐ There is inner tension within the individual between masculine and feminine parts of oneself. The resolution lies in finding harmony between the masculine and feminine within.

△ This person gets along with the opposite gender and is able to put creative expression out into the world.

♂ There is tension with the opposite gender, it seems to originate outside of one's self, even though the resolution of this tension lies within the individual in finding harmony between the masculine and feminine within. When there is harmony within, it is reflected in relationships with others, particularly of the opposite gender.

Sun/Mercury Aspects. ☉/☿

♂ Mercury never travels very far from the Sun, so it can only be conjunct in the natal chart. (In a transit chart, there are squares, oppositions, and trines.) Mercury is the messenger of the gods. He was always sent by the gods to deliver messages to humans as well as other gods. His is the story of Human Nature, half human, half god. Or another way to say it would be that humans have a spark of divinity. We are made in the image of God/dess. His mother was Human (Maia) and his father was a god (Zeus).

Mercury rules both Gemini and Virgo. The general rule is if Mercury is in a male sign, it brings out the Communicator aspects. For example, if Mercury is in Gemini or Aquarius, etc. then it is probably communicator. If it is a female sign (Taurus, Virgo, etc.), then it brings out the Soul Mother aspects. There are exceptions to this rule, so it is important to check it out with the individual whose chart is being read. Does this person have more Soul Mother qualities (attuned to nature, animals, being a healer) or Communicator (linking ideas, interested in communicating) qualities? They could have both also. It is also important to look at the whole chart in making a determination.

Mercury rules all types of communication. It puts an emphasis on one's friends, brothers, and sisters. Friends and siblings will be important if there is a conjunction to Mercury. It is a rather young, androgynous energy.

Sun/Venus Aspects. ☉/♀

♂ Venus can also only be conjunct to the Sun in the natal chart, because it is so close to the Sun. (Transit charts can have trines, squares and oppositions.) Venus is similar to Mercury in that it rules 2 signs: Taurus and Libra. The same rule applies. If Venus is in a male sign, it goes to Lover (relationships would be important). If it is in feminine sign, it goes to the Artist/Priestess (this would be a very creative person). As with Mercury aspects, there are exceptions to the rule, so it is important to check it out with the individual. Are they more artistic or are long-term relationships and marriage important to them?

Sun/Mars Aspects. ☉/♂

♂ This aspect involves 2 male energies. It will probably be a little bit easier for men to carry this energy than women. All the characteristics of the Warrior are emphasized here. Mars is also the athlete, which is difficult for women to connect to, as they aren't usually encouraged to be athletic. This will vary from family to family and also between cultures. Also there is more of an emphasis on girls and women's sports today than in the past.

---

[31] Dobbins, *Kabbalistic Astrology,* p.81

⁂ This emphasizes both the energies of the Warrior and the Golden Child, a dynamic energy if the person is comfortable carrying that energy. There would be a blending of personal power with soul mission. The immediate environment of the individual would reflect this; they would be a leader in their group of associates.

□ There is inner tension within the individual between personal power and life direction. This individual may become angry and frustrated when s/he is unable to achieve goals.

△ There is social harmony between personal power and life direction. People outside of oneself support one's direction in life.

☊ There is social tension between personal power and life direction. It feels like other people oppose one's power and direction in life. The resolution of this tension begins within oneself, to recognize one's own personal power and life direction.

Sun/Jupiter Aspects ☉/ ♃

☌ This aspect emphasizes the Teacher/Traveler aspect. Traditionally our school system has more of the wounded Elder Leader type of approach. Everyone learns by rote and memorization of facts; and everyone learns in the same manner. The Teacher/Traveler is more experiential, a hands-on teacher and learner. S/he likes to travel to other cultures to learn, to be there physically. This creates some tension with the traditional educational system. The Teacher/Traveler is also the spiritual teacher and leader, a guru of the community. The Teacher also does anything in a large, expansive manner. This is the Spiritual Father.

Since the Sun is very creative and fertile (produces children) and Jupiter is expansive, when these two planets are conjunct, there is a greater possibility of pregnancy.

□ There may be doubts about one's intellectual abilities to learn what needs to be learned. The mission is to work with those doubts within oneself.

△ This person does well in the educational system, and with spiritual traditions. S/he seems to receive encouragement from others.

☊ There is some tension between one's self and some teachers, the educational system; and /or some spiritual traditions or teacher. This person may have their own ideas that conflict with the teachings. They may feel compelled to leave the established group or community.

Sun/Saturn Aspects, ☉ /♄

☌ The archetype of the Elder Leader is emphasized. This is about becoming a mature leader, but with Saturn we have to work at transforming it in both our personal or professional lives. It is a very difficult energy. We don't do well with issues around power, authority, and leadership. We don't have much respect for authority. Think about dictators or leaders who haven't confronted their own issues. A mature leader would lead from vision, by setting an example on how to live one's life.

Even a conjunction with Saturn is difficult. It is a feminine energy, but it has traditionally been considered a father energy (father of authority). That's how far off base we are with this energy. The wounded side of this energy looks like the patriarchy: control issues, obedience without questioning authority, etc. The military exemplifies this energy. This model of course, makes the military more efficient on the battlefield, but doesn't encourage people to think on their own. The Elder Leader has a good work ethic.

⚹ Both the Golden Child and Elder Leader are leadership energies. They could bring together charismatic (Leo), mature leadership (Saturn).

☐ It feels like fatherly figures oppose life work and direction. There may be doubts about one's ability to work, perform, and create structure.

△ There is a working relationship with father and authority figures.

☍ There is separation from the father either physically or emotionally. The individual challenges authority or Father figures. This archetype can look like a rebel in youth when wounded,

Sun/Uranus Aspects. ☉ / ♅

♂ Uranus is the Father of Freedom. It is easier for men to carry this energy, as it is a male energy. This is Carl Jung's aspect. The personal mission is to lay out the Uranian mystery, which is about our time now. This energy deals with equality for all of humanity regardless of race, creed, gender, or sexual orientation. It is the dance of opposites: between masculine and feminine. Jung made us aware of the Self, which is a fully actualized, integrated person. Uranus is also very idealistic. Freedom is important and Idealists are often rebellious.

This energy is difficult for women to carry. The culture doesn't traditionally support women thinking on their own (Idealist energy), or becoming a distinct, opinionated individual. They are encouraged to conform.

⚹ Golden Child and Idealist are on opposite sides of the zodiac, but they are similar in that they are both dynamic male energies. The Golden Child performs more on an individual level, whereas the Idealist is involved at a cultural level. These 2 energies could bring together Idealism and creative leadership within the individual.

☐ There is tension between life direction, ideals, and one's relationship to changes. It looks like this person is always changing; they look Schizy, ungrounded. They don't get treated well by others; don't feel good about self.

△ One is able to bring ideals out into the world in a charismatic, dynamic way.

☍ There are unusual and different people in one's life. These people are eccentric and it feels as though they oppose you. Since this is the father of freedom, sometimes the father may be absent.

Sun/Neptune Aspects ☉ / ♆

♂ Neptune is nebulous, watery, mystical, unseen. It is the visionary. This individual will have a vivid inner life. S/he will be sensitive to psychic impressions, have vivid dreams. This person could also have spiritual experiences, although our culture doesn't support going directly to the Godhead. (Joan of Arc was burned at the stake because she maintained that God spoke directly to her.) The culture also doesn't promote being in touch with one's body or psychic processes. The Mystic wants to forget all of that and get lost in other peoples' processes. If you will remember, the Mystic has difficulties with boundaries. They project their experiences on others, and others project theirs on them. The Mystic needs to develop healthy boundaries and then they can connect with others. They also need to learn to trust themselves, to go within to find solutions, guidance.

✳ The soul's mission is to come to an understanding of the Mystic and begin to heal it. To be in touch with one's own psychic processes and model this health to others.

☐ There is inner tension about finding vision inside, but if don't trust self, it's hard to go inside.

△ There is an ability to connect with people, be in the world with this vision.

☍ The mission is to find a vision about human nature, but it is difficult if one doesn't trust oneself or others.

Sun/Pluto Aspects. ☉ / ♇

☌ This is an unusual aspect. We have the inner- most body of the solar system and the outer- most planet. The Dark Mother is the about the primal life force, the mysteries of life, sexuality, death, the unconscious, women's blood cycles. The patriarchy has connected women's sexuality with the devil, with luring men into sin. This is a deep, erotic archetype. The Dark Mother wants to plumb the depths, to explore the mysteries of life, death, and sexuality and will have a greater sensitivity to these issues than any other archetype. Dark Mother transforms whatever she comes in contact with. This is similar to the Baby Boomer era from 1938 to 1956 when Pluto was in Leo. There was a transformation in the way we looked at sexuality. "Love the one you're with seems to exemplify this, rather than the emphasis on monogamy of the previous generation.

✳ The soul's mission is tied to the Dark Mother. It depends on one's attitude to the body, sex, death, and the unconscious. The culture is going to oppose exploration of these topics.

☐ There is internal tension between the soul's mission and the Dark Mother. The mission is also to resolve this within oneself, to be comfortable with the life force.

△ Other people give support in bringing about understanding of the Dark Mother.

☍ The mission is to form a partnership with the Dark Mother, to honor her, heal her. That's the mission with any opposition. There may be a fear of the depths, but the mission is to go into those depths, to understand them, come to terms with them.

Moon ☽ (Nourishing Mother) Aspects

The moon represents our emotions, our deep inner life, our Mother, our primary relationships, family background, the children in our lives, relations to women and the feminine body. In the astrological chart, the moon represents the mother side of the family. The moon gives emphasis to any planet it is conjunct with. It is like a flashlight shining on that particular planet; it gives it an energetic, some importance. The Moon rules the 4th house. It is also a relational principle. The most intimate connection between 2 people is an ascendant-moon connection. That is when the sign of the ascendant of one is the same as the moon of another. This occurs between life-long partners and family members.

Moon/Mercury ☽/ ☿

Mercury represents communication, brothers, sisters and friends. With Mercury aspects, we must consider whether it is working more as the Soul Mother or the Communicator. Again the clue lies in whether the sign is in a masculine or feminine sign, and also with the characteristics of the individual whose chart is being read.

☌ If Mercury is in a feminine sign, the Soul Mother will be emphasized. This individual will be connected to nature and animals; perhaps they will have healing abilities (medical doctor, therapist, massage therapist, etc). They may possibly value their alone time, particularly in nature. The Soul Mother has more to do with wisdom or the way things interconnect in patterns than the Communicator.

If Mercury is in a masculine sign, the Communicator will be emphasized. This individual is more concerned with the gathering of different types of information and the expression of thoughts. The Communicator will also most likely talk a little faster, and exhibit more nervous energy than the Soul Mother.

☐ There will be inner tension with emotional expression -- or challenges to the physical body (moon), or immune and respiratory system (mercury). The Soul Mother has a wisdom wound. She represented feminine spirituality or Wisdom in the Old Testament until she was written out of it.

△ It will be easy to express ideas, emotions, or bring forth the healing aspect of the Soul Mother.

☍ It feels like other people inhibit our expression of ideas emotions, or healing abilities. As with all oppositions, it is important to address the beliefs within oneself and then the issues with others are lessened or disappear.

Moon/Venus ☽/ ♀

Again, this is similar to Mercury in that we need to determine whether we are working with the Artist/ Priestess or the Lover.

☌ Generally if Venus is in a masculine sign, it represents the Lover. This would bring out the Lover aspects; long-term intimate relationships would be important to this individual.

If Venus is in a feminine sign, then the Artist/Priestess would be emphasized and this person could have artistic abilities, an eye for beauty. They would desire beauty in their environment.

✳ If it is the Artist/Priestess, then there is the potential for a good relationship between Mother (Moon) and Daughter (Venus). Venus is a sister and daughter energy. It is a young feminine energy. It depends on the family background and the attitude toward relationships.

With the Lover energy, there is emotional expression of love between masculine and feminine.

☐ There could be tension within the individual regarding the mother or the family. The mission is to resolve this tension within, to come to acceptance of the situation or change it if possible.

△ There is the potential to blend together the young feminine and the mature feminine and the potential for great creativity.

☍ Feels unloved by the Mother and family. There are difficulties in relationships. Again, as with all oppositions, it is the mission to resolve this within oneself, and then relationships with others become easier.

Moon/Mars ☽/♂

♂ This emphasizes the Warrior energy: personal power, life direction, and athletic ability. The warrior is the athlete, who will likely stay active all of his/her life. Sometimes it is difficult for women to connect to this energy, to be physically active, and to express anger in an assertive manner.

✳ This would emphasis both the Nourishing Mother and Warrior aspects. There could be a good Mother/son (Warrior is a young energy) relationship.

☐ There could be conflict with women or the mother. Warrior energy influences one's own identity. There could be difficulty with one's self- identity; not being able to express oneself. The mission is to transform personal power in the family Soul. As we work on our own issues, we heal family issues also.

△ There is a generally harmonious relationship with the opposite gender. They would be good at physical expression.

☍ There is tension between the Great Mother and the Warrior. The Warrior is the one who did her in. The Great Mother culture was prevalent until 3500 B.C. The Earth and the Goddess were considered divine and respected. The warrior cultures conquered the more peace-loving, Earth-honoring cultures. Resolution of this aspect could bring power to the Mother aspect.

Moon/Jupiter ☽/♃

Jupiter aspects aren't that difficult, even the squares and oppositions. They have great potential to be resolved. Jupiter is an expansive, fun-loving energy. This energy is about belief systems. For example in therapy, we examine different beliefs that we have about ourselves, our country, our family, relationships, and then work to transform those beliefs that no longer serve us.,

♂ The Teacher/Traveler aspects are emphasized. This person will possibly be part of the educational system or be some sort of teacher, spiritual leader. They could also have difficulties with the educational system if they find it too rigid and desire a more experiential experience. They will also have an appreciation of other cultures and perhaps enjoy traveling. In fact that is how they learn best: drop out of school and travel for their education.

✳ There is an increased ability to work with and express beliefs.

☐ There will be struggles with the educational system, possibly coming from the family background. They may have difficulty belonging to a group, being independent, wanting to learn in their own way.

△ They will get along well in the educational system.

♂ There can be difficulties with teachers, the educational system, or certain
Spiritual traditions. The mission is to resolve this tension inside, resulting in acceptance of the group or founding a new group that better suits this individual.

Moon/Saturn ☽/♄

Where Jupiter is an easy, workable aspect, Saturn is difficult. It is about contraction, limitation, or absence. There is a heavy, depressive feel to Saturn. It is considered a father energy, even though it is in a feminine sign. It involves mature, cultural leadership. We don't have a very good relationship with power and authority. We tend to distrust authority from politicians to bosses. Saturn tends to dominate, control others. Even with a conjunction, there is a descent phase.

♂ This is a partnership of the 2 matriarchs. One (the moon) is the "woman of the house" and Saturn is the authority in the workplace. There is potential for development of mature leadership, both in home and the community. There is a mature emotional expression.

□ It feels like the father dampens emotional expression, ones femininity, whether this is true or not. The mission is to work within oneself, to value one's own emotional expression and femininity.

△ There is a harmonious relationship with the father, power and authority.

♂ There may be physical or emotional separation from the father. There is also a need to control others, sometimes through expression of derogatory comments toward the other. Remember this is a projection of one's inner tension on other people. The mission is to find one's inner authority.

Moon/Uranus ☽/♅

Uranus is the father of freedom. It is a rather erratic, unpredictable energy, sometimes the clown. This aspect combines feminine and masculine energy, so in some ways that makes it difficult, unless the person is comfortable incorporating those energies within oneself.

Most of the baby boomer generation (born about 1950-56) has Uranus in Cancer. They would exemplify this energy well, especially if they had an aspect with the Moon and Uranus also. This was the "flower children that questioned authority". They largely rejected the values of their parents and family (Moon). Uranus takes about 84 years to travel around the sun, which equals the average human life span. Uranus would typify three distinct stages in a life. For those born with Cancer in Uranus, they would typically separate emotionally from the family in first 28 years, reconcile with the family up to age 56 and then become a family fixture from the age of 56 to 84.

♂ This individual comes from an idealist family. It depends on the family background and how comfortable they are in the expression of ideals. Again this is an erratic, unconventional energy. It depends on whether one fights against that energy or embraces the idealism and the novelty within oneself. Also the mother may appear rather cool (a Uranian characteristic).

✳ This is ♀ similar to the conjunction, but not as difficult, in that there is a little more distance between the masculine and feminine principals. The conjunction involves working with these energies in a little more integrative manner.

☐ There is inner tension in expressing feminine identity (moon), whether that individual is masculine or feminine. The mission is to get comfortable with feminine energy, to see it as strong and not a weakness.

△ There is a comfort level and freedom of expression of the feminine in a social manner.

☍ There may be a separation from the family or mother. There is a desire for freedom of expression or in relationship. Given freedom, people with this archetype will return to the mother or family.

Moon/Neptune ☽/ ♆

These two energies are much alike. They are both watery, feminine signs. Both are impressionable, psychic (Neptune more so), and sensitive.

☌ This was Carl Jung's aspect. This person comes from a Mystical family, especially on the mother's side. There is potential to be a visionary, to tap into the soulful depths. Altered states of consciousness are attractive, so the individual must make sure they do that in a healthy manner and not with substance abuse.

✳ This would be a creative and artistic combination.

☐ There is fear of the depth realm, of looking within oneself; to do so one may go crazy. Again Neptune is such a deep, soulful energy, but we are discouraged from being too introspective. We don't trust our inner selves. We think we will go crazy if we gaze within too long. The mission is to go within, find guidance there.

△ There is ability to vision on a broad, social level, to be intuitive.
☍ There is a tendency to see craziness in others. Relationships are a fog. There are boundary issues with others. The mission is to be able to clarify boundaries, to be able to verbalize one's feelings in order to separate out one's feelings from others.

Moon/Pluto ☽/ ♇

These two energies are also similar; both are watery, emotional, feminine energies. The Dark Mother is intense, connected to emotional depths: the life force, death, and sexuality. The Nourishing Mother is expressive.

☌ The Dark Mother energy is emphasized because of the conjunction with the moon. There is an ability to connect to erotic depths. This is a deep, intense energy. It can be very secretive and private. A lot will depend on the way the family background works with this energy. A family who attempts to understand and talk about life, death, and sexuality will have an easy time with this energy. To avoid a topic is to just create an obsession with it. It becomes wounded and gets expressed in a wounded manner. The most wounded aspect of the Dark Mother is sexual abuse: incest, rape, or preoccupation with pornography. This avoids developing the Dark Mother aspect into a mature partnership with another mature person. This was Carl Jung's mother's aspect. Some would say there was a deep, intense almost crazed look in her eyes. There is an intense depth to the eyes of people who carry Dark Mother energy. One is pulled into the depths.

☐ There is a fear of losing one's self to passion, to the inner wounded anima. There can be suspicion, not wanting to go too deep within oneself. The mission is to go into those depths and be comfortable with them.

△ There is Comfort with and an ability to connect to and express deep erotic depths.

♂ It feels like others are preventing one from going deep. The other person changes the subject is when the topic becomes too deep. The mission, of course, is to allow oneself to go to those depths, to honor the inner life. Again, our society tries to gloss over sensitive subjects, rather than go into them, experience them. Death is a good example of this. We often put a time limit the grief period. We expect someone "to get over it and move on"

We can't do that unless we fully go into the experience and allow ourselves to be sad.

Mercury ☿ Aspects

Mercury represents both the Communicator (masculine) and the Soul Mother (feminine). It will depend a lot on whether Mercury is in a feminine or masculine sign.

The Communicator deals with all types of communication, electrical systems, siblings, and one's earliest environment. It is a young, androgynous energy.

The Soul Mother is a more Mature energy and slower and deeper at processing information. She is the Wisdom aspect, where as the Communicator is the information gatherer. She will also be connected to nature and animals and there is a deep connection to Service to humanity.

Mercury (Communicator)

Ruled by Mercury in Gemini. It is a mutable (changing) air sign. Air represents mental energy. This is the transition sign between spring and summer. Mercury is quick, revolving around the sun faster than any other planet. Traditionally it was the messenger of the gods.

Mercury (Soul Mother)

Ruled by Mercury in Virgo (or perhaps really the Earth if we were to change the astrological system). It is the Soulful, Spiritual feminine energy. It signals the end of summer, the transition to autumn.

Mercury/Venus ☿/♀

♂ There is the possibility of several combinations here. Venus also rules 2 signs: the Artist Priestess (feminine sign) and Lover (masculine sign). With the Communicator and Artist/Priestess aspect, there is creative communication or writing; siblings are important in one's life. Soul Mother and Artist would be a little more practical, physical creativity: weaving, sewing, gardening. It could also be a creative healer. They are both Earth signs. The Communicator and Lover would be an expressive lover. The Soul Mother and Lover would be a practical, perhaps healing relationship.

The following aspects of Mercury/Venus would only be possible in a transit situation, where one of the planets on a given day was in aspect to the other planet in the natal chart. Since Mercury and Venus travel so close to the Sun, they are never very far from each other. These aspects are short-lived however as the planets travel a relatively short distance around the Sun.

□ There is a writer's block, inner tension with creative expression or expression of healing abilities or communication within a relationship. The mission is to work with and resolve this tension within.

△ There is an ability to express creatively out into the world or a creative way to heal others. There is expressiveness within a relationship and with siblings.

♂ It feels like siblings oppose one, or there is tension with siblings. Also others oppose one's creativity or healing ability. The mission is to allow one's creativity to flourish.

74

Mercury/Mars ☿/♂

These are both young, masculine energies (if Mercury is in a masculine sign). Both have a lot of nervous energy: Mercury is verbally expressive and Mars is physically active.

♂ There is the ability to express thoughts in an innovative manner. There is good mechanical ability (Mars). If Mercury is working as the Soul Mother, this would be an innovative healer, provider of service to others. Mars rules the adrenal system and Mercury the respiratory system

☐ There is volatile, angry communication; also accident prone around cars (Mars). The mission is to learn to express oneself assertively rather than aggressively. Tension could get locked in the body, in the respiratory system. There could be difficulty in expressing oneself. The mission is to work with these energies within oneself.

△ One is innovative in the expression of thoughts to other people.

☌ It feels like people, siblings (Mercury) don't understand what one is communicating. The mission is to work with this tension within oneself, so that you can communicate more fluently to others; also to be patient with others if they don't seem to understand.

Mercury/Jupiter ☿/♃

Here are two masculine energies if Mercury is working as the Communicator (in a male sign). Mercury rules communication and Jupiter belief systems, so they can work well together. Jupiter also expands any energy it is in contact with.

♂ This person is a gifted communicator, maybe a little too much as it can be overdone. This could also enhance one's healing ability, connection to service if Mercury is working as the Soul Mother.

☐ There may be doubts about one's intellect, ability to perform in school, especially if it is a Soul Mother aspect. The mission is to recognize one's intelligence and abilities.

△ This is an expressive and persuasive speaker; one who would be comfortable in front of a group of people, able to work with other's belief systems in order to enable others to understand one's point of view.

☌ May have difficulty sharing one's thoughts. The mission is to work with this perceived disability within oneself; to put self in situations where you can practice communication and develop it so one is comfortable communicating with others.

Mercury/Saturn ☿/♄

Again Saturn restricts, limits energy it is in contact with, but it gets easier as one gets older. Saturn also rules time, both young and old.

♂ There would be an ability to express oneself in a mature manner. If Mercury is working as the Soul Mother, there would be a mature healing ability. They are both Earth signs. There could be a restriction in communication, but it could be worked through as one gets older. Even in a conjunction there is a mini descent.

□. There is a break down in communication. There is possibly tension with brothers, sisters, and friends. The mission is to keep attempting to communicate, look at the manner in which it is communicated.

△ There is expression of mature authority. Others respect and listen to one.

☍ There is a power struggle and difficult communication dynamics with authority figures or with the father. Again, look at the words, content, tone of one's expression.

Mercury/Uranus ☿/ ♅

These are also two male energies if Mercury is working as the Communicator. Both are also nervous, active energies.

♂ This is a fast talker; a very, bright, innovative communicator, but they make leaps of intuition that others may not be able to follow. Sometimes they can talk so fast that others have a difficult time understanding them. Uranus rules the nervous system and Mercury the respiratory system. There is a lot of tension and stress that inhibits the respiratory system, but there is an ability to work through this, as Uranus is able to change quickly and dramatically. Often times Uranus can look like a chameleon.

□ There is a lot of tension, anxiety that gets locked in the body in the respiratory system. There tends to be shallow breathing and difficulty expressing ideas. It would be helpful to this person to practice deep breathing exercises, to practice speaking more slowly and precisely.

△ Is able to communicate ideals to others.

☍ It feels like friends, siblings oppose, don't understand one. The 11th house (Uranus' house) also rules friendships. This person will have to work extra hard at explaining ideals to friends and siblings.

Mercury/Neptune ☿/ ♆

♂ Here we have a conjunction with the rational (Mercury) and intuitive (Neptune). It depends on how Mercury is working (Communicator or Soul Mother). The Soul Mother would be more compatible with Neptune, would be able to communicate about the other- worldly realms.

□ If it is Soul Mother, there is a fear of being crazy; lots of doubts and confusion about being intelligent. Neptune or the Mystic has a fear of one's own inner processes, that they really are crazy, that these thoughts and ideas are an illusion. The mission is to honor one's intelligence and intuition.

△ This can be a very powerful and intuitive communicator, able to use sensitivity to communicate.

☍ Has difficulty forming a union, partnership with friends and siblings. They don't understand. There is a fear of looking crazy. The mission is to honor one's intuitive processes, to be able to express this.

Mercury/Pluto ☿/ ♇

Pluto is a deep, intense energy. It rules the life force, death and sexuality.

☌ If Mercury is working as the Soul Mother (in a feminine sign), it can be a very intense, sensitive healer. This is the aspect of Midwifes hospice workers, therapists and other healers. If Mercury is working as the Communicator (male sign), there is an ability to communicate about these erotic depths, life, death, and sexuality.

☐ There is a fear of talking about the erotic depths, of being able to look at them, a fear of being pulled into them. The mission is to address these issues, to be able to look at death and be comfortable with the life force.

△ One is able to express sensitivity about the deep mystery realms: also would be an expressive healer.

☍ It feels as though people don't understand one's depth and sensitivity. The mission is to honor one's sensitivity and be able to express it. Often we feel like others shut down our expression. We internalize that aspect and we also "shut down" our own sensitivity and expression.

Venus ♀ Aspects

Venus (like Mercury) represents 2 archetypes: The Artist/Priestess (feminine) and the Lover (masculine).
Both archetypes value aesthetics and beauty in their surroundings.

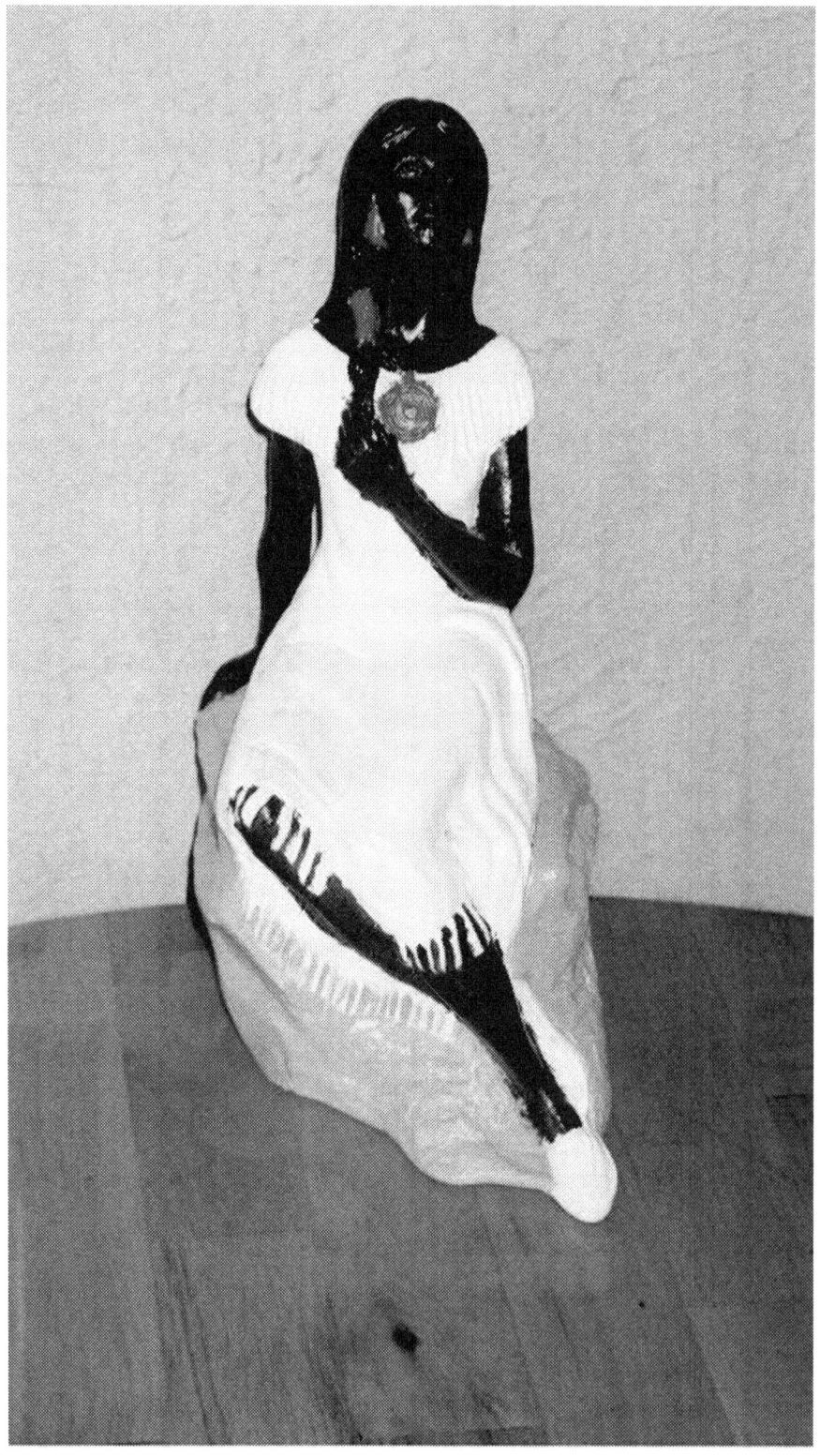

Venus (Artist/Priestess)

78

Ruled by Venus in Taurus. It is a fixed Earth sign. It rules the second house and concerns things of beauty and value. This is the middle of spring. This energy is very creative and artistic. It becomes very frustrated if not allowed to express this creativity. The Artist/Priestess is creative, sensuous, erotic, aware of creative mediums, and experiences life through the 5 senses. It is a young feminine energy, a daughter energy. Also, sister relationships characterize this archetype. There was a sisterhood among the artist/priestesses in Innana's temples in Sumeria (See the 12th Planet by Zecharia Sitchin). Inanna was also the sister of Ereshkigal (the underworld was her realm). The Patriarchy down graded the artist/priestesses to temple prostitutes and shamed them for their sexuality. It was even thought that they were consorting with the devil. Since people with this archetypal energy are naturally very erotic, they tend to draw attention to themselves.

That can be very overwhelming in our culture because it is often believed that women particularly are doing something to attract that attention. Their partners can be very jealous. Or men wounded in their own expression of sexuality will be attracted to them and behave inappropriately. The Artist/Priestess has a lot of issues with the body. The Patriarchy considered Lover being in the physical body not as important as spiritual pursuit, especially anything of a sexual nature. Women with this archetype sometimes take on the shame and think there is something wrong with them; they are ashamed of their eroticism and sexuality. They try to compensate by giving away their power to their partner. Also they naturally like attention and physical contact and can be very vocal when they don't receive it. There is a tendency to gain weight as this archetype is attracted to sweets.

Venus (Lover)

Also ruled by Venus in Libra. Lover is a male, air sign. It is cardinal as it is the beginning of autumn. Libra is opposite of the Warrior or Aries on the zodiac wheel. Where as Aries seeks personal power, the Lover seeks fulfillment in another. There is a drive to relationship. This is the Lover's Spiritual mission; to obtain the balance of Yin and Yang in relationship. He sees his lover as a mirror of himself/herself. This energy can become wounded when there is a need to always be in a relationship or to totally run away from it so as to not deal with issues related to relationship.

Venus/Mars ♀/♂

♂ This represents lovers and conception, the blending of masculine and feminine in a harmonious way. If the Artist were emphasized, this would blend the creative aspect with personal power, to be able to bring forth those creative aspects in a personal and powerful way. Many artists are very creative, but one must also be a marketer (Mars), to get one's work noticed by others.

□ There is tension within the individual between the inner masculine and the inner feminine. There is loss of creative self. Can't say what one wants to say because one loses personal power; there is tension between relationship and personal power. One has to work with expressing self to partner, get them to listen.

△ There is harmony between masculine and feminine relationships. This is a good aspect for singers, dancers, creative people, and the ability to put one's work out into the public view.

♂° There is tension in relationships. It feels like others oppose one's creative endeavors. It is important to honor's one's creativity and be able to put it out in the world, even when it feels like others don't appreciate it.

Venus/Jupiter ♀/ ♃

Jupiter expands on the characteristics of any planet it is in aspect to. It also represents the Spiritual Father, the teacher, the guru and love of other cultures.

♂ This would enhance the relationship life. There would be a lot of opportunities to expand one's circle of friends. There is an abundance of creativity, artistic expression. There is love of the Spiritual Father, teacher, or Guru, and of learning and travel. Since Jupiter expands, there is the possibility of weight gain.

□ It feels like one's social life is shut down. The mission is to work with this repression inside, to put self in situations where you can learn social graces, to expand one's creativity.

△This is the Social Butterfly, the partier. Jupiter can get carried away; it may need some limits at times.

♂° It feels like others shut one down. Possibly there is difficulty with the educational system, certain teachers or belief systems. The mission is to work with one's creativity, find schooling experiences that are relevant to one

Venus/Saturn ♀/♄

Saturn, again, structures and constricts. It is also insightful to notice what house Saturn is in. There will be a limitation or difficulty or absence in the qualities that the particular house represents. For example, in the 7ᵗʰ house, it would represent limitation or difficulty with relationships. It is also an elder energy, so that relationships may be easier as one gets older. The elder is sometimes serious when young and then more light-hearted as they mature. Although Capricorn is a feminine energy, it has been traditionally considered a father energy. That is how far off base we are with this energy. In the patriarchy, the emphasis is on masculine, not feminine qualities. Saturn is considered the father of structure. There is a heavy, depressive feel about Saturn, but it can be worked through.

♂ There is a love of the father, but it is difficult to get to because anything with Saturn takes extra work. But the rewards are also great.

□ There is a sense within oneself that the father or parents (elders) don't love one, whether this is true or not. The mission is to develop appreciation for oneself, the authority within.

△ There is a love of the father; this can be healing for both the father and daughter. In our society, there is uneasiness in many father/daughter relationships. Especially as a girl becomes a teen and she naturally pulls away from her father, and all of the emotions of hurt, jealousy associated with that.

☍ Possibly there is a physical or emotional separation from the father. The mission would be to find a surrogate father or one's mature authority within.

Venus/Uranus ♀/ ♅

♂ Similar to Moon/Uranus, the relationship life will look different—this aspect will have lots of idealism, change, wanting freedom and transformation. There may be multiple relationships with an obsessive Uranian search for the ideal, perfect relationship. Uranus is the ideal dance of the opposites—between masculine and feminine. We are to help each other develop. It is the myth of our time. But since no person or relationship is perfect, it is hard to obtain, and the person may just give up on relationships. The mission is to accept that relationships are less than perfect and require work. There is also a need for freedom in creative expression. It is difficult for these 2 energies to work together, even in a conjunction because one is feminine and one is masculine and there is such idealism, but Uranus is very changeable, so it is possible. There is a descent process even with a conjunction.

□ There is an internal need for freedom, change, and creativity. For women it's difficult to express creative ideal; it's hard to paint it, dance it or sing it. It gets locked up in the body, in a high-strung, anxious Uranian kind of tension. For men it's hard to get in touch with the creative aspect, so they look cool, distant, and heady.

△ Both planets are relationship principals. Men will identify more with the Uranian side, women with the Venus side. The goal is to make each other whole. This is new dance of the opposites (Uranus). It's possible to break through and create relationship with this aspect.

☍ There is possibly an absence of the Father or lover. It is easy to idealize someone who is gone. It is also difficult to find someone who meets one's ideals. Even the Gods and Goddesses had their shadow sides in mythology. Again the mission is to accept that relationships are less than perfect.

Venus/Neptune ♀/ ♆

♂ This is a mystical union. It is similar to Venus/Uranus, but without the freedom issues. The Mystic (Neptune) is the greatest projector of all the archetypes, constantly seeing the problem out there in other people, not in themselves.

☐ There is shadow material around the Mystic—illusion and mistrust. Women will have difficulty in finding center around their body, sexuality, sensuality, and identity as a woman (Venus). The mission with the Mystic is always to take the projection back inside and work with it within.

△ There is an inner creative ability to bring this out in relationship life.

♂ There is illusion in relationship; can't see what's going on in the relationship life. It is important to check out the issue with one's partner. "This is what I think just happened here. What do you think happened?"

Venus/Pluto ♀/ ♇

♂ This is the Dark Mother and Daughter (Venus) joined at the hip. There are deep, passionate dynamics around the erotic, sexual body. These two energies are the most erotic and sexual. There may also be deep, ugly fears around sex. A young girl who carries this energy will carry erotic energy in her soul; sometimes wounded people are attracted to her. Cocaine could be a dimension of this aspect, as the Dark Mother likes the intense roller coaster ride of cocaine. There is a famous male ballet dancer with this aspect, who is addicted to cocaine. Dancers are often in a lot of pain, so there is a temptation to use cocaine to numb the pain. In the end, it just makes it worse. The body develops a high tolerance to cocaine and other medications become ineffective.

☐ It is difficult for women to connect with erotic, sensual part of themselves and feel good in the world. Education about Dark Mother aspects helps women diminish the shame and accept themselves for who they are.

△ One is able to integrate lover and sexual being within self and bring it out in the world.

♂ There is opposition between lover (Venus) who wants connection, and union and the seductress (Dark Mother), who wants sexual union. The goal is to bring these 2 together.

Mars ♂ (Warrior) Aspects

Ruled by Mars in Aries, the spring sprout l sign of spring. It is cardinal sign, the initiator. Aries occupies the 1ˢᵗ house or the ascendant. The ascendant represents one's personality, identity, how one presents to the world.

Mars (the Warrior) represents personal power, life direction, and the ability to pioneer change. It is a very physical energy, very passionate, and assertive. Mars can work with any type of energy or any planet it comes into contact with. It is the physical energy behind a project. It gives a spark to any planet it comes in contact with. The other planet contacted by Mars will determine which project will be initiated.

Mars/Jupiter ♂/ ♃

♂ These 2 energies work together well as they are both masculine energies. The warrior is willful, active, fiery, and dynamic. Jupiter deals with beliefs and is the Spiritual father or the guru. This is the warrior/teacher, an innovative guide with a broad understanding of the dynamics of the world. This individual will have a dynamic teaching style, although anything can be overdone and Jupiter can over-teach, be too enthusiastic, which can irritate others. There can be conflicts in teaching situations.

□ There are beliefs in one's life that inhibit one's ability to find one's own identity. Mars is sensitive to self-esteem and personal identity. Many men tend to externalize their pain, so that when they get hurt, they deny the feeling of pain and vulnerability, and then they get angry and attack others. The mission to develop one's own identity, work with the pain within, rather than project it on others.

△ This can be a powerful, innovative teacher, able to bring this teaching out into world.

♂ It feels like teachers, spiritual leaders, or one's own father is threatened by one; they oppose one's personal direction. The mission is to recognize that one's own identity and personal power resides within and is not dependent on others.

Mars/Saturn ♂/♄

♂ This is a personal power (Mars) and control (Saturn) dynamic. Power and control are associated with domestic violence. Both planets rule the physical body and both are wounded. Mars is the athlete, ruling the muscular system. Saturn rules the structure, the skeleton of the body. Ideally they could bring together mature authority and youthful vitality.

☐ There is internal tension within one's self between personal power and authority. One may also be prone to car accidents (Mars aspect). Since this aspect attracts power and control, the police will be out in full force during these cycles or if we are driving erratically, they will notice.

△ This person is able to take mature authority and youthful vitality out in the world.

☍ There is a conflict with old power systems (parents, father, boss, etc). It feels like those in authority oppose one. Or when one gets older, it feels like young upstarts oppose you. There is a heavy depressed feeling emotionally and also present in the body

Mars/Uranus ♂/ ♅

♂ This brings together the ground- breaker in Mars and the changer in Uranus. This brings forth new ideals about healing the body since Mars is a physical energy. This is a body healer. This person needs freedom in life and in relationships.

☐ There is tension in the body regarding the respiratory system and pituitary glands (Uranus rules both of these areas). This person is also restless. These two archetypes are probably the most energetic and have trouble sitting still for very long.

△ There is an ability to express ideals in the world in a unique, physical sense with force and power.

☍ There is difficulty in putting ideals out in the world. This individual could feel a lack of physical energy in expressing these ideals; or they put out ideals, get anger back from others. Uranus is an androgynous energy so certain macho men might think this individual is gay if this is a male. The mission is to resolve the inner conflict between personal power and ideals and then opinions from others may change or aren't as hurtful.

Mars/Neptune ♂/ ♆

♂ This is the Mystical Warrior or Spiritual fanatic as the Warrior can overdo things. The fog of war could also describe this aspect, as with Mars in Neptune from June 17, 2003 to December 16, 2003, the people of the United States seemed to question the lingering of the Iraqi war after the quick "march" to Baghdad. Martial arts and Yoga would be of interest to them. Neptune is the visionary.

☐ The Mystic is tapped into the collective unconscious (unconscious processes of all the people of the world) and will periodically cycle through the depths of emotion as they ride the waves of the collective unconscious. They are like the lightning rod of the world. The Warrior feels energy move through his or her body. This person will often feel surges in body of the collective unconscious. There is a fear of craziness, of looking within oneself (Neptune), and yet that is what one must do and to learn to trust self.

△ There's an ability to bring mystical, artistic power out into the world.

♂ One's personal power opposes mystical beliefs within one. The person can't be mystical and be in the body (a shadow Neptunian belief). The Warrior is very physically oriented and the Mystic likes to be out of body. They don't feel very grounded. The mission is to ground this mystical vision and take it out into the world.

Mars/Pluto ♂ ♆

♂ Dark Mother (Pluto) is the sexual, feminine body and Mars or Warrior is the athletic masculine body and can also be aggressive and impulsive. There is rape, anger, and attack on the Dark Mother out of fear. Many men become angry when they are afraid, and then they attack. They can't linger, get close to the deep feminine energy, or the depth realms. We have a fear in our culture of the depth realms. These two could work together in an innovative way to empower the Dark Mother. There is a descent process even with a conjunction, but also an ability to heal and resolve this.

□ There is going to be an inner tension within the person between the deep feminine sexual expression (Pluto) and the power dynamics of the Warrior resulting in difficulty managing energy in the body. The Warrior tends to be impulsive, impatient with a deeper process. The mission is to acknowledge the Dark Mother and all her awesome power and to express it in a physical sense.

△ This is an innovator in understanding the body and depths of the Dark Mother. They are able to transform people with touch. There is tremendous leadership ability and erotic, sexual power. Both aspects are leaders. Many political leaders have Dark Mother energy.

♂ One gets intensive response from people who see one as too physical and too sexual. There can be attack from people who fear the Dark Mother energy. The relationship life is going to be physical and volatile (Mars). The mission is to resolve this conflict within regarding personal power and sexual expression. Others will mirror that expression, then.

Jupiter ♃ (Teacher/Traveler) Aspects

Jupiter represents one's belief system, education, travel, and spiritual groups. It is the Spiritual Father, the Guru. Jupiter is expansive. It thinks big. Jupiter aspects are not that difficult, even the squares and oppositions. It is a very benign planet. It is opposite Gemini on the astrological wheel. Whereas Gemini is concerned with gathering data and Sagittarius is concerned with synthesizing beliefs to their highest meaning.

Jupiter/Saturn ♃/♄

♂ The ancients called this a Syzygy. It occurs approximately every 20 years. (For a more in-depth explanation see Kabbalistic Astrology: The Sacred Tradition of the Hebrew Sages, by Rabbi Joel C. Dobin, D.D.) The Hebrews believed that the Prophets channeled wisdom from the Gods. This brings together the mid heaven cosmic energies. Saturn is the farthest planet that can be seen with the naked eye. It transmits the message of God to Jupiter, who in turn transmits it to the inner planets. Saturn would represent Yahweh (structured) and the prophet or Spiritual Guru (Jupiter). There is a possibility of liver difficulties with this aspect, as Jupiter rules the liver.

□ There could be tension in the individual between old traditional beliefs (Saturn), possibly from the family and higher, deeper beliefs (Jupiter). The person will be in process in trying to resolve this conflict and examine beliefs around spiritual matters.

△ There is an ability to bring prophesies from a higher source into the world; to bring together mature authority and spiritual beliefs and philosophy of life.

♂ There is tension between beliefs and those in authority. There could be difficulty with groups of people (Jupiter); one might try to control them (Saturn). The mission as always, is to resolve this conflict within oneself.

Jupiter/Uranus ♃/♅

♂ There are a lot of similarities between these two male energies. Both are revolutionary, into higher thought, and group oriented. This would be a very brilliant teacher, with creative mental abilities. There is a tendency, however, to overdo teaching; to be ultra-idealistic, and to dominate the group. This is just something to be aware of.

□ It could be an inner tension with being part of a group and possibly some tension with teachers. It could be difficult to change, to get clear on one's goals. There is an inner tension with flying or travel. The mission is to resolve this inner tension between teachings and a need for idealism.

△ There is a good group facilitator with an ability to work with groups of people, and to possibly take this out on the road (travel).

♂ There is tension with peer and educational groups and this person may leave the group in a dramatic (Jupiter) way. Uranus is eccentric, freedom loving, oppositional, which sometimes can look dramatic. This person may feel outside of the group, like one doesn't fit in. S/he can either explore these differences with the group or may end up leaving.

Jupiter/Neptune ♃/♆

♂ This is the mystical teacher. Both of these energies are teachers; they are both integrative and holistic. They can be very inspiring, channel beliefs from the unconscious; receive visions about new direction in life. Jupiter is more rational. The mission is to let go of some of the rational part and trust self (Neptune).

□ There is tension within the individual regarding Neptune's lack of trust of oneself, of being able to contact the depths. It's difficult to teach about those beliefs around the mystical, the unconscious. There can be confusion, conflicting beliefs. This person may find education challenging. The mission is to resole these conflicts within oneself.

△ There is an ability to put inspired spiritual teachings, one's philosophy of life out into the world and possibly on the road. The teacher is comfortable in small group settings.

♂ Sometimes this person can look lost, have difficulties with ones relationships or educational background. It's possible to receive vision from the other people in the world. This aspect is not that difficult; it is workable. This is an opposition between fundamental religion (Jupiter) and the more mystical traditions like Christian and Jewish mysticism and Sufism in the Muslim tradition. This aspect is currently occurring (June 2003). Notice the tension between fundamental Muslims and the idea of democracy, which ideally should embrace all people (Neptune).

Jupiter/Pluto ♃/♇

♂ The Soul mission is to present the teachings about the Dark Mother and the primal life force to the world. Primal life force involves birth, death, sexuality, and the reproductive cycles. It is a deep, soulful energy and involves transformation and healing. It's important to become comfortable with talking, teaching about these subjects. The mission is to heal, transform the Dark Mother, possibly through some writing or teaching.

▢ There is inner tension about beliefs around the Dark Mother. It's difficult to get to the depth realms. One needs to change one's beliefs about spirituality, the educational realms.

△ There is an ability to take these teachings on the road, to educate small groups. This would also make a good banker, to be able to work collectively with money. Scorpio traditionally involves working with other people's money.

♂° There could be opposition from certain people regarding the primal life force, sexual and reproductive issues. This could affect one's relationship life. The mission is to resolve the issue within one's self and therefore transform one's relationship life.

statue by Abby Willowroot

Elder Leader

Saturn ♄ (Elder Leader) Aspects

Where Jupiter expands, Saturn contracts. It is opposite of Cancer on the zodiac wheel. Where as Cancer is the home, Capricorn is the work environment. Saturn represents structure, a strong work ethic, and mature leadership. It represents cultural leadership, as in tribal, city or neighborhood. It is also the father of structure, even though it is a feminine energy. In its patriarchal aspect, it is controlling, operates out of fear. This is where it is wounded, off base. It feels depressive, heavy.

Saturn/Uranus ♄/♅

♂ This combination would be a challenge. We have Saturn, which is foundational, structured and Uranus, unstructured, revolutionary, and changeable. Could bring new ideals about the myth of the opposites (Uranus) into the culture (Saturn). This could make for a good scientist. Uranus is inventive and Saturn enjoys working within a structure, with set formulas.

□ There is inner tension between old and new beliefs, which would manifest in the body as anxiety. There is tension in the body between structure, the skeletal system (Saturn) and the nervous system (Uranus). There is the possibility of these two energies working together to bring ideals to the culture.

△ There is an ability to express ideals and goals out in the world in an inspirational way, to be a ground-breaker with mature leadership abilities.

♂° One feels at Odds between old, traditional beliefs and new beliefs around the Uranian mystery, the dance of opposites. There is opposition from more conventional types of people. If the person could resolve these issues internally, it would change one's environment and the people in it. Sometimes we have to remove ourselves from an unhealthy environment.

Saturn/Neptune ♄/♆

♂ This is the Mystic and Elder Leader. It's challenging in the patriarchal society to bring these 2 together. There is a fear (Saturn) of the depths of the Collective Unconscious (Neptune), which could develop into deep mental problems. It feels like the emotions get in the way. There is also the possibility of bringing a unitive (Neptune) understanding to the culture (Saturn).

□ There is a fear of the depths of the collective unconscious (Neptune). Cultural beliefs interfere with Neptune's visionary abilities. The Mystic naturally moves through cycles in which visions and dreams arise from the Collective Unconscious. There is also cyclic depression as The Mystic is able to touch those emotional depths, and there is also a lot of pain in the collective unconscious. The patriarchal culture doesn't understand these visions and Saturn reacts with fear to anything it doesn't understand. It tries to control it. (Remember Joan of Arc was burned at the stake for her visions and her belief that she could talk to God.) It is important to develop trust of oneself and of the inner voice.

△ There is an ability to bring broader social understanding into the world, lead with vision. Not many political leaders lead from vision, they just try to stay in power by satisfying the majority of people. This aspect occurred in the early 1940's.

♂° There is opposition between the visionary (Neptune) and the practical side (Saturn). The tendency is to repress the visionary because you can't trust it. This person draws a lot of resistance when one tries to go deep in relationship. As with all oppositions, the tension originates within the individual, but it draws resistance from other individuals. The goal is to balance this out within oneself.

Saturn/Pluto ♄/♇

♂ There is a strong cultural leadership; very magnetic, could span over different cultures, such as several countries or tribes. This aspect was prevalent in 1947.

□ There is tension between the deep, passionate life force (Dark Mother) and structured authority (Elder Leader). Again the mission is to blend the positive qualities of these two archetypes within oneself, in order that they may work together. There could also be some difficulty with the immune or reproductive system (Dark Mother), and the skin and bones (Elder Leader).

△ There is potential for practical leadership as both are leadership principles,

♂ These are 2 leadership styles opposing one and another: One is structured (Saturn) and the other is deep and charismatic (Dark Mother). One draws opposition from others. The mission is to bring together these two energies within oneself.

Idealist (statue by Michael Garman)

Uranus ⛢ (Idealist) **Aspects**

Uranus has an unusual rotation; spinning on it's side.   It is opposite Leo in the zodiac wheel. Idealist is more community oriented, where as Leo is more personal. We stepped into the Uranian age in 1981 with the conjunction of Jupiter and Saturn, also known as a Syzygy. Carl Jung brought forth this Uranian mystery in his writings. It is the myth of our time, a new understanding, a dance of opposites. Uranus is freedom loving, revolutionary, and eccentric. This is the father of freedom. It is a fixed, masculine air sign, even though it is the water bearer.

Uranus/Neptune ♅/ ♆

♂ These two energies would work together well. There is visionary idealism, the ability to touch the metaphysical, and altered states of reality.

□ There is an inner inability to translate visions and ideals. The mission, as always with Neptune is to be able to go within oneself and to trust those visions.

△ There is an ability to bring visionary idealism to humanity.

♂ Uranus is very cerebral and Mystic is emotional, other worldly. This plays out in relationship life. One feels opposed in expressing this mystical, idealism. The mission is to balance the mystical vision with the intuitive leaps of the Idealist and to bring this out into the world and into the relationship life.

Uranus/Pluto ♅/ ♇

♂ This is characteristic of the 60's – free love. There is a loosening up the passionate mysteries of life, death, and sexuality. There is idealism around how these two could operate in the world.

□ There is an inner tension between the passionate life force (Dark Mother) and idealism. The love life can be erratic. It is important to become comfortable with the Dark Mother energy and let it express through oneself.

△ There is an ability to bring about new ideals regarding the life force and present them to the world.

♂ There seems to be opposition from others regarding ideals and the life force and sexual life. The mission is to resolve these issues within oneself. There is then more harmony in the relationship life.

Neptune ♆ (Mystic) Aspects

Neptune is the visionary, receiving dreams, images, and emotions from the Collective Unconscious. It is difficult to trust these nebulous images in a society that values solid, material proof. People who act on instinct and hunches are questioned. Pisces is a feminine mutable water sign. It is opposite Virgo. Both are concerned with humanity; Virgo in a more practical, physical sense and the Mystic in a more spiritual, emotional sense.

Neptune/Pluto ♆ / ♇

♂ These two could work together well as they are both emotional, sensitive energies. There is an ability to visualize the connection with the life force.

☐ There is a process around the immune system producing an inner tension. (The Mystic, Dark Mother, and Soul Mother all have sensitive immune systems because of their psychic abilities to attune to others.)

It is important to establish healthy personal boundaries so as to not take on others emotional baggage. Also some physical exercise helps ground and balance this emotional aspect.

△ This person can bring forth collective, charismatic vision to the social realms.

♂ Initially there is tension in relationship life, but with work there is an ability to bring about new vision regarding the primal life force and how it relates to life, death and sexuality.

Pluto ♇

(Dark Mother)

This is the queen of the underworld. It is deep, intense energy, concerned with the primal life force of life, death and sexuality. It is opposite Taurus in the zodiac. Both are erotic and sensual. Taurus is more physical and Scorpio is deeper, more intense and emotional.

Mid-life Aspects

There are also some astrologically aspects that occur at middle age, which is from the age of 37-42. These are listed below.

♇ □ ♇ Occurs between 37-38 years of age. Relates to ego/body issues. There can be a major illness and recovery, requiring the person to examine lifestyle. This relates to the Dark Mother (Pluto). Pluto is a transformational energy and relates to the body, reproductive cycles and the life force. It can feel like a part of us died, was healed and transformed.

♅ ♂ ♅ Occurs between 39-40 years of age. There is an emphasis on relationships with the opposite gender (divorce, separation), career goals, ideals, and life mission. Idealist concerns are highlighted with issues of idealism, changes, and freedom in relationship. There is a restructuring and transformation of one's relationship and ideals in life.

♇ □ ♆ Occurs between 41-42 years of age. It relates to the Mystic and issues around spirituality and envisioning one's life in a new way. There is a new Spiritual awareness, "a new vision of the way life works". There is integration in presentation of the Self in the World.

Interpreting the Aspects in Baby Jane's chart.

Now we will look at Baby Jane's chart again with a view to the aspects between the planets in her chart. I found that in looking at the aspects in her chart, they mirrored the story told by the ruling archetypes. In other words, you could figure out the ruling archetypes and have a fairly good idea about the chart without looking at the aspects. One advantage of understanding aspects is that you can look at the transits and get a good idea of what the person is currently going through.

☉ □ ♅ Sun squaring Uranus: Jane is Idealist and this is another aspect of that energy. She may have some inner tension between her ideals and life direction. As she gets older, she may have certain ideals about how the world should work, but have difficulty putting those ideals in action in a meaningful direction in her life. She may appear to change often and will look ungrounded by others. She may not get treated very well by others and so not feel very good about herself.

☉ △ ♆ Sun trine Neptune: Jane should have the ability to take the deep-soul Mystic vision out into the world and present it to others as part of her Soul Mission, particularly since she is a Mystic herself

☽ ☍ ☿ Moon opposite Mercury: She may feel that others inhibit her expression of ideas or emotions.

☽ △ ♂ She will have good physical expression of her emotions and she will get along with the opposite gender. (Watch out Dad.)

☽ ✳ ♃ She will be creative at expressing her beliefs and may have some good experiences within the educational system.

☽ ☍ ♇ She may feel like others inhibit her expression about the depth realms; keep her from going deep.

☿ ✳ ♆ This is the rational/intuitive connection. She should be able to express the deep soul mysteries in a manner that others understand.

♂ ✳ ♃ She will have a dynamic teaching style.

♂ △ ♅ She will be able to express ideals in the world in an energetic, dynamic way.

♃ △ ♇ She will be able to take the teachings to the road. She would also be a good banker. Pluto is good at handling money at a society level.

Conclusion

Hopefully, the readers were able to grasp a basic understanding of Jungian Archetypal Psychology as developed by Charles Bebeau Ph. D. This is a beginning. There is so much information to learn about this whole topic. We are revisiting Feminine Spirituality and Psychology as practiced by ancient people when the Earth was the all-providing Mother. We are stepping into the Aquarian Age, the dance of opposites of feminine and masculine. We are developing new relationships between all of humanity and a new respect for human rights, where everyone can develop their human potential. This may be a few years away, but we have taken the first steps. We are on cutting edge of the Aquarian Age and hopefully this book will help you down that path. I feel privileged to be part of this journey.

There is also a web site that you may access for more information. It is www.jungianarchpsych.com

About The Author

Theresa Bauer, LPC, CAC III is a Jungian Archetypal Therapist, getting her certification from Avalon Jungian Archetypal Institute in Boulder, Colorado. She has been in private practice for 14 years and works with adolescents, families and substance abuse clients. She has a son who is a Navy aviator.

Elizabeth Cox, M.A. attended Avalon Jungian Archetypal Institute in Boulder, Colorado, where she received her certification as a Jungian Archetypal Therapist. She is a teacher and a therapist working with families, adolescents and substance abuse clients. She has 3 grown children, who are artistically inclined.

www.ingramcontent.com/pod-product-compliance
Lightning Source LLC
Chambersburg PA
CBHW080421290526
45791CB00008BA/2366